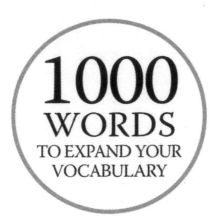

1000
WORDS
TO EXPAND YOUR
VOCABULARY

By the same author:

The Story of English
Symbols
The 25 Rules of Grammar

1000
WORDS
TO EXPAND YOUR
VOCABULARY

JOSEPH PIERCY

Michael O'Mara Books Limited

First published in Great Britain in 2018
by Michael O'Mara Books Limited
9 Lion Yard
Tremadoc Road
London SW4 7NQ

A CIP catalogue record for this book is available from
the British Library.

Papers used by Michael O'Mara Books Limited are natural,
recyclable products made from wood grown in sustainable forests.
The manufacturing processes conform to the environmental
regulations of the country of origin.

ISBN: 978-1-78243-891-5 in hardback print format
ISBN: 978-1-78243-899-1 in ebook format

1 2 3 4 5 6 7 8 9 10

www.mombooks.com

Designed and typeset by Ed Pickford

Printed and bound by CPI Group (UK) Ltd, Croydon, CR0 4YY

Introduction

When I was young, really young, my parents were worried there was something wrong with me because I didn't speak very much. When I did speak I was afflicted with an overt stammer. The words I wanted to say just couldn't be spoken quickly enough, the thoughts that I had couldn't be expressed exactly, or nearly exactly, how I wanted them to be. In short, I didn't have the words to say what I wanted to say. Hence, I fell silent, withdrew into an internal world, until I learned to read and discovered more words and ways to hide my stutter.

I've been involved in the meaning of language (and the language of meaning) for well over half my life. In order for a language to function it needs two components: a vocabulary and a grammatical structure. Grammar is sexy in my opinion, a puzzle and a trick, smoke and mirrors maybe? Vocabulary is far more mundane, possibly? After all, it is only words? Right? Wrong!

The beautiful thing about the English language is that it is the most expressive and descriptive language in the world. English absorbs words, like a giant sponge; words from all different cultures that it chews up, swallows and spews out again in different forms; it's a Leviathan, the Kraken, a ravenous Hydra – basically it's a monster, but a beguilingly beautiful beast.

So how do you choose a thousand words from this linguistic maelstrom? Well, I hold my hands up and confess my decisions were partly based on words I like, partly on words I had no idea what they meant and partly on words I thought sounded cool and interesting. There are thousands more out there swimming around in the whirlpool waiting to be hooked out, so please don't take this as an exhaustive list by any means.

It has been an interesting journey. There are lots of words in this book which I have been using erroneously, 'mordant' being one of many. Equally fascinating are the peculiarities of common speech: 'I locked myself out of my house last week but happily my neighbour has a spare key.' Actually, my neighbour did not appreciate being woken up at 3 a.m. to give me the spare key at all and so didn't happily let me get into my house. *Haply* (fortuitously/luckily) my neighbour has a spare key to my house, but who would notice the difference? But there is a difference in meaning and that is important. Ambiguity is the enemy of truth and meaning and therefore, rather worryingly, general understanding.

It's a slight point, maybe, but worth considering nonetheless. Increasingly, we live in a world of 'fake news' and 'the post-truth epoch', and thus the necessity to express what we really want to say is of paramount importance; to speak, write and communicate as clearly, concisely and correctly as we can. And for that we need the right words. It is to be hoped this little book may help in some small way.

Joseph Piercy

A

Aberrant: If something is aberrant it is deviating in some fashion or manner from the norm. Aberrant is a direct borrow from the Latin word *aberrāns*, meaning to go astray. A secondary meaning relates to behaviour, specifically bad behaviour or behaviour considered out of character or abnormal.

Such aberrant behaviour will not be tolerated.

Abet: To encourage or assist another in the fulfilment of an action or (often illegal) activity.

She was charged by the police with aiding and abetting a bank robbery.

Abeyance: In English the word abeyance can be used in technical legal language and in a more generalized manner. Disputes over the contents of a will, for example, may cause a property or title to be placed in abeyance, meaning waiting to be claimed by a rightful heir or owner. Future plans can also be in abeyance if they are dependent upon the outcome of a change in future circumstances.

We had to put our plans for a camping trip in abeyance due to a sudden change in the weather forecast.

Abjure: To abjure is to reject, renounce or forswear a belief, practice or opinion. The word shares the same Latin root *jurare*, meaning to swear an oath, as perjury and jury and hence has its groundings in law. It is possible of course to casually abjure any formerly held belief or opinion, but in the Middle Ages if the Spanish Inquisition demanded someone abjure from ungodly practices or beliefs it usually meant being tortured or burned at the stake. Not to be confused with adjure (see below).

He abjured his devotion to soccer when it became so expensive to attend matches.

~

Abnegate: A verb that shares its Latin roots with several other words, all of them in denial. *Negare* means to deny or refute and the word abnegation began to appear in English as early as the fourteenth century. It was, however, several hundred years before abnegate appeared as a verb. This is an example of retroactive word formation, as it is natural to assume that the act of denying occurred before anyone was accused of being in denial. Abnegate can also be used in a formal sense to refer to the relinquishing of power or responsibility.

President Obama rushed several bills through Congress before protocol decreed he abnegate his presidential powers.

~

Abrogate: A potential malapropism with the previous entry, as in some senses abnegate and abrogate are very similar. To abrogate is to take authoritative action to abolish or annul something, whereas to abnegate is to give away authoritative power. Where it all gets a bit murky is when it comes to abnegating or abrogating moral responsibility for actions, but that is a matter for subjective judgement.

The incursions by rebel forces had forced the government to abrogate the fragile peace treaty.

~

Abscond: A borrowing from the Latin word *abscondere*, meaning to conceal or hide. People usually abscond in a hurry; typically to avoid detection of or an arrest for an unlawful action such as theft.

They absconded with the weekly bar takings and fled to Spain.

~

Abstemious: The words abstemious and abstain are often thought to be synonymous but in fact they derive from different Latin roots. To be abstemious is to deny oneself the joys of intoxicating drinks as the Latin root noun *temetum* means, basically, booze. The Middle English/Anglo-French word *abstinēre*, however, means to hold back from or refrain. One can abstain from anything but only an abstemious person refuses a drink.

Many people like to play at being abstemious, especially in January after weeks of self-indulgence.

~

Acarpous: An Anglicization of the Greek word *karpós*, meaning fruit. *Karpós* is steeped in Greek mythology. In English, the addition of the prefix *a* as a negation gives us a word meaning simply, without fruit or barren. The word can also be used as a synonym for sterile or unfruitful in a figurative sense.

After four hours the board meeting was becoming distinctly acarpous as not a single decision could be agreed upon.

~

Accoutrement: Often used in plural form, accoutrements are extra or additional items used for some purpose (not always strictly necessary). Derived from Old French, the word originally referred to personal items soldiers carried with them. In modern parlance, accoutrements are often regarded as fashionable items – accessories such as hats, gloves, handbags and jewellery. Quite where the connection between the military and high fashion was formed is anybody's guess, except perhaps for the fact that French soldiers were generally well dressed and conscious of their appearance.

The major wore all the accoutrements of his rank: sash, medals, ceremonial sword and, frankly, a quite silly hat.

~

Accumbent: To be in an accumbent position is to be lying backwards and reclining. The word derives from the Latin *accumbere*, meaning to lie down or lean back. Historically the term is the name given to the habit of eating while lying horizontally, as depicted in classical art and sculpture. It is questionable if the habit of the ancients adopting the posture while feasting was due to some misplaced medical ideas about digestion or was merely (and more probably) just an affectation of wealth and decadence.

The frieze depicts the Emperor Nero, in accumbent posture, being tended to by a gaggle of concubines.

~

Acedia: Derived from the Greek word *kēdos*, meaning care or grief, with the negative prefix *a* it translates as lack of caring. The word acedia in English was originally closely related to the sin of sloth and, as such, became synonymous with laziness. Over time, however, the meaning has become more associated with apathy or boredom.

By Sunday he'd succumbed to acedia and stayed in bed until lunchtime staring at the ceiling.

~

Aciform: A botanical term used to describe certain plants, aciform derives from the Latin noun *acus*, meaning needle. The word can be employed to describe anything that is shaped like or resembles a needle, such as the spines on a porcupine, or figuratively for anything that is sharp and spikey.

Her aciform personality made her work colleagues wary of her.

~

Acquiesce: To acquiesce first arrived in English in the seventeenth century via the French word *acquiescer*, meaning to remain at rest or to rest satisfied. However, its more modern meaning of to accept something without protest or to accede to the will of others comes from one of its earliest recorded uses in the writings of the philosopher Thomas Hobbes. In his famous work *Leviathan* (1651), Hobbes argues that strong government can only be achieved if the people 'acquiesce' to the rule of the sovereign and the guidance of the Church – that is, accept without question decisions made on their behalf. A more subtle variation of usage is people being forced to acquiesce reluctantly because they have no viable alternative.

'Our Beleefe … is in the Church; whose word we take, and acquiesce therein.'

Thomas Hobbes, *Leviathan* (1651)

∼

Acuity: A complex word and one which needs to be used carefully. Acuity relates to the human senses and mental perception and in this context can be used as a synonym for the more common word sensitivity. To have strong aural acuity is to have very sharp and accurate hearing. To have mental acuity is to be perceptive and insightful.

Serious head injuries can often have serious side-effects on the acuity of the senses.

∼

Acumen: Acumen in modern usage means to have a depth of perception or keen grasp and insight into a subject or area of knowledge. The word is closely related to acute as both stem from the Latin word for needle, *acus*. In the fifteenth century acumen related mostly to having quickness of mind and sharp wits and gave rise to the phrase 'as sharp as a needle'.

Due to his mathematical acumen, and skill with numbers, he could solve in minutes complex problems that took other students several hours to understand.

∼

Adjure: A curious verb and its infrequent usage says much perhaps about the modern world. Although closely linked to other words such as importune and implore, adjure is much more earnest in nature and heralds from a time when people listened to each other more. To adjure is to solemnly advise somebody on a course of action. People who importune tend to be quite pushy and people who implore quite needy. People who adjure are more balanced, cautious and wise.

My liege, I adjure thee to reconsider this course of action.

∼

Adumbrate: Adumbrate is a word much beloved of academics, particularly historians and literary critics. Derived from *umbra*, Latin for shadow, an action can often adumbrate or foreshadow another future action or consequence. In literary narratives, for example, one action adumbrates a further development in the plot. Adumbrate is also sometimes used in the sense of overshadow.

The prophecies of the three witches adumbrate the fate of Macbeth.

∼

Aestivate: The antonym of hibernate, aestivate is the practice of spending long periods in a sleep-like state of torpor during summer or hot dry seasons. Certain species of fish, amphibians and insects in the world aestivate when water supplies diminish.

As a point of pedantry, creatures don't hibernate in summer, they aestivate.

∼

Affiche: A rare word that arrived in English via French. An affiche is a printed, often illustrated notice displayed in a public place, often promoting an event such as a concert or art exhibition. In French there are all sorts of elegant-sounding variations, such as *affiche de cinema* (film poster) and *affiche lumineuse* (neon sign), and to be top of the bill or the headline act is to be *tête d'affiche*.

The original 1960s affiche de cinema *are highly collectable.*

∼

Affluence versus Opulence: Affluence describes a person who has become wealthy, either by accident or design. Opulence is a more general term for an abundance of wealth and resources. Therefore the oil-rich states in the Middle East are opulent societies where affluent people reside.

It wasn't until I moved to Dubai that I really experienced affluence, as I had never lived anywhere so opulent.

∼

Agglutinate: To agglutinate is to form by joining together as if by glue. The word is fairly recent, with its first recorded usage being at the turn of the twentieth century. Originally used in biological terminology when describing the grouping of blood cells, the process of agglutination is also a linguistic term for forming compound words by, literally, sticking them together.

Karl Landsteiner identified different blood types after observing how certain cells agglutinated with others.

~

Agiotage: A polite term for a rather grubby business, agiotage is the practice of exchanging different currencies in order to make a profit. From the French verb *agioter*, meaning to speculate, the word first appeared in English in the early eighteenth century and was often applied to Jewish moneylenders/bankers, so has vaguely anti-Semitic undercurrents.

On the streets of Moscow the practice of agiotage was rife during the financial upheavals of the early 1990s.

~

Agog: Agog derives from the Middle French words *en gogues*, meaning to be in good humour. It also has links to the verb to goggle, meaning to stare with intense interest and excitement. When we are agog we are viewing something with wide-eyed interest.

The boys were all agog with the presents they received for Christmas.

~

Alacrity: Derived from the Latin word *alacer*, meaning lively and enthusiastic, to display alacrity in action is to show cheerful readiness and willingness. Alacrity shares similar roots to the musical term *allegro*, which denotes a jaunty tempo. Jane Austen and Shakespeare were fond of the word, with the latter's Richard III, on the eve of the Battle of Bosworth, bemoaning his lack of energy and verve.

'I have not that alacrity of spirit,
Nor cheer of mind, that I was wont to have.'
William Shakespeare, Richard III, Act 5, Scene 3

⌇

Albescent: To describe something as albescent isn't quite the same as describing the colour white. Derived from the Latin *albēscere*, meaning to turn white, it refers to the process or appearance of something whitening or shading into whiteness.

Her face took on an albescent hue when she heard the terrible news.

⌇

Aleatory: *Alea* is the Latin word for dice or playing games with dice as in the famous phrase attributed to Julius Caesar, *Alea iacta est*, or 'the die is cast'. A situation is aleatory if it is at the mercy of random factors and chance, like the roll of a dice. The word is often used to describe unfortunate happenings or unpredictable results.

The picnic was ruined due to the aleatory nature of the weather.

⌇

Aliment: Aliments are vital, we couldn't survive without them. In Latin, *alimentum* means food and nourishment and other elements needed to sustain life; in English, aliments are anything that we need for healthy survival. The word is the stem for alimony in divorce law, which are the payments needed for the support of a spouse (and family) following the dissolution of a marriage.

He went in search of the aliments needed to survive in such a barren environment.

⌇

Altruism: The practice of altruism is doing charitable acts for the benefit and welfare of others. The word is an Anglicization of the French word *altruisme*, which has the same meaning and developed from *autrui*, meaning other people.

Mother Teresa was canonized for her life of devoted altruism.

⌇

Amaranthine: A beautiful adjective steeped in poetic suggestion, amaranthine has its roots in the odes of Ancient Greece. *Amarantos* in Greek means immortal or undying and this gave rise to the mythical flower the amaranth, a flower which never wilted or faded.

The adjective amaranthine, then, refers to anything that is immortal and timeless.

The amaranthine beauty of the sun setting over the sea.

~

Ambages: An archaic word that is seldom used and yet has survived in English since the fourteenth century. An ambage is a winding or indirect pathway or route. Ambages are inconsistencies or lack of clarity in something and it is from the Middle English *ambages* that the word ambiguity derives.

The plot was littered with deliberate ambages and false leads designed to perplex the reader.

~

Ameliorate: This word derives from the Latin word *melior*, meaning better, and although broadly synonymous with better and improve there is a subtle distinction in usage between the words. In general we can only ameliorate a situation that is bad to begin with, making it more tolerable. We can make things better and improve things that aren't bad to begin with, such as our standard of living or general health and well-being.

The government's intervention helped ameliorate the dire consequences of the financial crisis.

~

Amorphous: Derived from the Greek word *morphē*, meaning form, amorphous is used to describe something without clear or distinct form. The word is often used in association with sprawling shapes devoid of clear lines, such as clouds. A secondary use is in describing things that are without a definable character or nature.

He stared up at the amorphous clumps of clouds drifting past.

~

Amphigory: Amphigory is nonsense or gibberish; there is no point looking for meaning because there isn't any. It derives from the French literary term *amphigouri*, which was a style of burlesque poem or song popular in the eighteenth century. The word amphigory in English can be used to describe written or spoken language that may seem on the surface to be meaningful but actually makes no sense.

Edward Lear was a famous writer of amphigories.

~

Anachronism: An anachronism is something out of its own timescale or an error in chronology relating to objects, events, customs or people.

Eagle-eyed movie buffs love to spot anachronisms in historical films, such as an actor wearing a wrist watch hundreds of years before they were invented.

~

Anadiplosis: Anadiplosis is a rhetorical device – one that repeats itself for emphasis and impact. Often used by speech writers and politicians, the key to effective use of anadiplosis lies in repeating a memorable phrase at the beginning of a sentence. Classic examples of anadiplosis are Civil Rights activist Martin Luther King's 'I have a dream' speech and Winston Churchill's 'We shall fight them on the beaches' speech.

But you must know your father lost a father. That father lost, lost his, and the survivor bound.

William Shakespeare, *Hamlet*, Act 1, Scene 2

~

Anagoge: A word with strong spiritual implications. Derived from Late Greek, the root word *anagōgē* denotes something lifted or raised upwards. The word is most commonly associated with theology and relates to a mystical interpretation of a sacred text that aims to reveal meanings beyond the literal, traditional or allegorical readings.

The trendy new priest was particularly fond of turning his Sunday sermons into an anagoge by using obscure words and citations.

~

Anathema: Anathema has had a rather chequered history. The original Greek word related to anything that was devout or a holy offering. This could often include anything, person or object, that was used in the name of God in some way. At some point, however, anathema also came to mean any object used in a holy war, such as the weapons of the enemy. This was seized upon by religious authorities, who started cursing objects, and gradually the original meaning of being devout became, in the eyes of various religions, being devoted to evil and wrong-doing. The modern sense of anathema is any thing, person or concept, that an individual finds repellent and intolerable.

Prejudice in all its different forms was anathema to him.

~

Anchorite: Taken from the Greek word *anachōrein*, meaning to withdraw, an anchorite is an old-fashioned word for a hermit. Anchorites were often, but not always, religious minded and withdrew from the world to live in quiet contemplation.

Gaudí became an anchorite in the latter years of his life and lived alone in a hut beside the Sagrada Familia cathedral.

~

Anodyne: Anodyne comes from the Greek word for painless. This accounts for the fact that anodynes in noun form are things that relieve pain. As an adjective, though, anodyne is often used negatively to describe something so insipid and bland that, although unlikely to cause offence (or pain) it is just as likely to bore someone to tears.

Much mainstream music in the 1980s was so anodyne it's a wonder anybody listened to it.

~

Antecedent: In grammar an antecedent is a word or phrase replaced by a substitute, usually a pronoun. A principle of fine writing is to keep antecedents clear and unambiguous. For example, in the sentence: 'Rosa does her mother's shopping every week but she doesn't appreciate it', it isn't clear if 'she' refers to Rosa or her mother. The secondary meaning of antecedent is something that has gone before, usually a condition or event that has had an effect on the future.

The antecedents of the Great War can be found in Germany's growing economic isolation from the rest of Europe during the late nineteenth century.

∽

Antiquarian: An antiquity is something that is ancient, particularly dated before the Middle Ages. First coming into use around the beginning of the seventeenth century, the term antiquarian denotes a person who collects, studies or sells valuable old things.

He was an antiquarian of great renown, having published a number of books on the subject of the ancient Persian Empire.

∽

Aphorism: Although the word aphorism entered English via the Middle French word *aphorisme*, its origins date to Ancient Greece. The great physician Hippocrates of Kos (460–370 BC) is thought to have first coined the word *aphorismos* in his medical writings on disease. In the strictest sense, an aphorism is therefore a definition or a diagnosis. Over time, however, the word has come to mean a self-contained, often pithy, statement of generalized truth such as 'less is more'.

Nietzsche's later writings abandoned philosophical models in favour of sharp dazzling aphorisms.

∽

Apoplectic: Originally, apoplectic related to the medical condition of apoplexy or having a stroke. A more common use of the word is to describe someone so enraged they can barely speak; they are stunned with fury (as if having a stroke).

His controversial speech left many of the audience apoplectic with rage.

∽

Apotheosis: The Ancient Greeks were particularly fond of creating gods, and the origin of the word apotheosis comes from this practice. *Theos* is the Greek word for God, hence apotheosis means to create gods. In more modern secular times an apotheosis, while retaining some elements of divinity, has come to mean an ultimate example of something or a perfect form.

James Joyce's Ulysses *is regarded by some critics as the apotheosis of the modernist novel.*

∼

Appellation: Appellation is a noun for a noun. The Latin verb *appellare* means to call or summon, and in most cases it helps to know the name of someone (know their appellation) when trying to attract their attention.

I go by the appellation Joe with my friends and family.

∼

Apprise versus Appraise: The French verb *apprendre*, meaning to learn, provides the root for apprise. Although closely synonymous with inform, apprise is used to impart specific information, often in relation to an ongoing situation. Inform has the meaning of introducing new information. To appraise means to assess or examine the qualities, values or needs of something (or someone).

The prime minister has asked to be apprised of the ongoing situation.

I was asked to appraise my staff by Human Resources.

∼

Arboreal: *Arbor* is the Latin word for tree and has given rise to lots of tree-related words. Arboreal as an adjective means relating to or resembling a tree. The elegant but rarely used verb arborize can be used to mean something that is branching outwards, either literally or figuratively.

The proliferation of beautiful trees around the park were the fruits of the late duke's arboreal passions.

∼

Arcadian: Arcadian derives from the Greek province of Arcadia. In antiquity, Arcadia had a reputation for being an unspoiled and pastoral idyll whose inhabitants lived a simple and peaceful existence at one with nature.

He moved to the countryside to pursue a stress-free Arcadian lifestyle.

~

Arcane: If something is arcane it is shrouded in secrecy. This is because arcane derives from the Latin word *arcanus*, meaning confidant or trusted friend. The word is often misused; when we talk about arcane rituals of the Aztecs, for example, we are saying that these rituals are obscure and knowledge of them is highly specialized – we aren't, as is often assumed, describing them as ancient.

The Freemasons is an organization steeped in arcane rules and rituals.

~

Archaize: To archaize is to make something appear to be old-fashioned or from a different time. The verb relates mostly to the arts (fine art and literature) but is often used to describe design (especially fashion) and architecture.

The high neckline is a deliberate attempt to archaize the overall effect of the dress.

~

Arenaceous: A seemingly docile adjective with a strangely violent history, arenaceous is anything made of or containing particles of sand. In botanical terms, arenaceous plants grow best in sand rather than soil. The word, however, derives from the Latin *arena*, sand-filled spaces where gladiators fought their battles and raced their chariots. Arena in turn derives from the Latin *harena*, which was the name for the fine sand used there on account of it absorbing blood.

Cacti and agaves are examples of arenaceous plants.

~

Arraign: In legal terminology, to arraign somebody is to call them before the court to answer a charge or indictment. The word, however, has existed since the fourteenth century and derives from the Middle English word *arreinen* meaning to address in an accusatory fashion.

He was arraigned on account of non-payment of parking fines.

～

Arrant: Arrant is a distortion of the word errant, which at o..e time was used to describe a wanderer or a vagabond, as in the errant knights of medieval times. Something that is arrant is usually bad – an epitome or out-and-out example of badness. Shakespeare was fond of the word and uses it in several of his plays.

'The moon's an arrant thief and her pale fire she snatches from the sun.'
William Shakespeare, *Timon of Athens*, Act 5, Scene 3

～

Arriviste: A relatively youthful word that has only existed in English since the turn of the twentieth century. Borrowed from the French verb *arriver*, meaning to arrive, an arriviste is the new kid on the block. The word has slightly negative connotations in some usage. Arriviste is often used to describe someone who has appeared from seemingly nowhere and is disturbing the old order of things.

His first major exhibition cemented his position as the arriviste of the New York art scene.

～

Asinine: To speak or behave in an extremely stupid or foolish manner can be described as being asinine. Derived from the Latin word *asinus*, a secondary meaning of the word is to display features or characteristics of a donkey (ass), animals traditionally thought of as being stubborn and stupid.

'Never assume, it makes an ass out of me and you,' is an asinine thing to say.

～

Assiduous: Derived directly from the Latin verb *assiduus*, meaning to be constant, assiduous has come to be seen as a virtue, roughly synonymous with unremitting and persistent. In Ancient Rome the word had a variety of different uses, one of which was to be fixed in position or location. In English, for a time, assiduous was often used to mean over-eagerness to please in a social sense. However, we now use it to mean dedicated to detail and cause.

He was an assiduous collector of rare books and manuscripts.

~

Assuage: To assuage is often quite complex in English as its usage is very subtle. The word derives from the Middle English *aswagen*, meaning to sweeten something. In modern usage to assuage is to make a situation or state less intense and more tolerable. A secondary meaning is to satisfy or quench a particular need or desire.

He partially assuaged his guilt over forgetting his mother's birthday by sending her a bouquet of flowers.

~

Asthenia: 'It is a good life as long as you don't weaken', as the saying goes – that is, suffer asthenia. From the Greek word *asthenēs*, meaning weak, asthenia is a generalized medical term for fatigue.

One of the side-effects of working night shifts is abnormal sleep patterns that can lead to general feelings of asthenia during the day.

~

Atrabilious: Atrabilious traditionally described someone who was prone to bouts of melancholy. Ancient Greek medicine defined the 'four humours' of human metabolism that they believed were essential for maintaining good physical and mental health. An imbalance in the humours caused issues in physical and mental well-being. Melancholy derives from the Greek words *melan* and *chole*, meaning black bile. Greek medicine had a strong influence on medieval Europe, and in Latin atrabilious derives from the words *atra* and *bilis*, which translates also as black bile, the substance thought to be the cause of mental strife. The meaning of atrabilious has changed, however, in modern usage and the word is now often used to describe somebody who is tetchy, irritable and short-tempered.

Family gatherings were always spoiled by Grandma's atrabilious behaviour towards her grandchildren.

❧

Avuncular: A rather quaint and heart-warming adjective, avuncular means simply 'uncle-like' in character or behaviour. This does of course presume that all uncles are kindly and reliable souls with only the best interests of their nieces and nephews at heart. There isn't an adjective for a bad uncle.

A sweet and avuncular man, he was much beloved by the local community.

B

❧

Bacchanal: Bacchus was the Roman god of wine and fertility (equivalent to Dionysus in Greek mythology). The feasts of Bacchus known as The Bacchanalia were riotous assemblies in Ancient Rome, wild orgies of unabashed hedonism replete with goat-skinned headdresses and wild dancing women. A bacchanal is therefore either a particularly wild and drunken party or a person devoted to decadent and unrestrained behaviour.

Errol Flynn was the first of the Hollywood hell-raisers, a bacchanal who threw notorious parties on his private yacht.

❧

Bailiwick: In medieval England a bailiff was a local sheriff who had legal jurisdiction over a certain region, village or town. This was known as a bailiwick. By the nineteenth century, bailiwick came to be used in a figurative sense to describe a person's area of expertise or sphere of influence.

The Russian Revolution was the professor's notable bailiwick.

❧

Balbutiate: The tendency to balbutiate is an unfortunate and frustrating affliction. From the Latin word *balbutire*, meaning to stammer or stutter. The word is virtually obsolete in modern usage other than in academic speech and language journals and the novels of the writer Will Self.

My uncle has a tendency to balbutiate when he becomes excited.

≈

Baleful: A word which has been around in English for over a thousand years, baleful derives from the Old English *beolofull*, meaning evil or wicked. Over time the word has come to be used to describe portents of something bad – in demonology and studies of the occult, *Balam* is a three-headed prince of hell.

She shot him a baleful look of barely disguised malice.

≈

Ballyhoo: A ballyhoo can be either a loud commotion in a crowd of people, such as a public meeting or demonstration, or exaggerated publicity and excitement drummed up by advertising.

There was much ballyhoo about the new Star Wars *film.*

≈

Baneful: Baneful is very similar to baleful and also has its roots in Old English, with *bana* being the word for murderer or destroyer. The subtle difference between the usage of the two words lies in cause and effect. Whereas something baleful is suggestive of something unpleasant, baneful is the destructive consequence.

Scientists have long predicted the baneful effects of climate change on the planet.

≈

Baroque: The word baroque entered into English from French, where originally it described something that was irregular in shape, particularly gemstones. In the mid-seventeenth century the baroque art movement in design and architecture utilized extravagant curved lines and ornate and complex decoration. As a result, baroque can be used as an adjective to describe something that is elaborately designed or constructed.

The style of the novel is baroque, filled with complex descriptions and long, lilting sentences.

~

Bate versus Bait versus Abate: To bate something in the traditional sense was to lessen the intensity or force of something. The base verb form has more or less disappeared from usage but has been replaced by the phrase to wait with 'bated breath', which means becalmed anticipation or excitement. The verb to bait is to try to make angry with criticism or insults, or to entice into a situation such as an argument or dispute. The verb abate is similar in meaning to the now scarcely used 'bate' in that it has the sense of to reduce in degree or intensity or to wait for a situation to become more moderate or palatable.

He attempted to bate my fury with soothing words.

I take every opportunity to bait my uncle over politics.

We took shelter in an old wooden shack and waited for the storm to abate.

~

Bathos: Bathos is largely a literary term coined by the poet Alexander Pope to describe the sudden switch from a serious or intellectually pertinent subject to something trivial or commonplace.

Many critics were bemused by the ending of the film, feeling that the sudden bathos of the dénouement masked the serious message.

~

Batrachian: From the modern Latin taxonomy *batrachia*, which is used in zoology to describe species of amphibians. Batrachian can also be used as an adjective to describe anything resembling a frog or toad in appearance or behaviour.

Despite her protestations, many commentators believe the prime minister has filled the Cabinet with batrachian 'yes men'.

~

Bawdry: A bawdry person is someone who uses coarse and obscene or sexually suggestive language. This was not always the case, however, as the word derives from the Middle English word *bawd* or *bawde*, meaning a prostitute or somebody who ran a house of ill-repute. A further obsolete usage was to describe a woman who was unchaste, but this probably died out because losing one's chastity didn't necessarily mean being a prostitute.

Shakespeare's comedies are full of bawdry jokes and allusions.

∾

Beano: In the nineteenth century an employer would throw an annual party for his employees (usually a meal with entertainment) known as a bean feast. Over time bean feast was abbreviated to beano and developed a general meaning for a party or celebration.

She got very drunk at her work's annual beano and made a fool of herself on the dancefloor.

∾

Beatitude: Beatitude is from the Latin *beatus*, meaning happy. Beatitude is a state of high and unremitting bliss. In theology the word relates to any of the blessings given by Jesus in his Sermon on the Mount as recounted in the Gospel of Matthew and so beatitude can mean a divine blessing bestowed upon somebody.

A feeling of beatitude befell him as he lay lounging in the bath.

∾

Befuddle: A relatively new word in English, to befuddle means to become disorientated and confused. Originally, the word related to the effects of excessive alcohol consumption and, in particular, the practice of opium smoking in Victorian times. In modern usage, to befuddle someone is taken to mean a deliberate attempt to perplex or distract.

He became rapidly befuddled as the evening wore on.

∾

Belabour: The verb to belabour has two meanings, both linked to repetition. The sixteenth-century meaning was to repeatedly strike something or someone, as to belabour blows with a hammer or belabour punches upon an opponent in a fight. The more modern sense suggests something far more tedious: people belabouring the points of an argument by going on and on and on …

The government continued to belabour their stock argument over the economy to such an extent that it no longer has any impact.

~

Bellicose: To be bellicose is to be inclined to start fights or, more specifically, wars. The word first appears in Middle English via the Latin word *bellum*, meaning of war or warlike. In the twentieth century the word was often applied to various despots and dictators such as Hitler and Mussolini in reference to their political speeches and expansionist policies. In general, however, bellicose can be used to describe any aggressive action designed to provoke conflict of some kind.

The bellicose comments by the president have made the United Nations uneasy about the events in North Korea.

~

Bemire: Taken from the Middle English word *mire*, meaning a bog, which in turn was borrowed from the Old Norse word *myrr*, to bemire, in a literal sense, means to become covered in mud. The word can also mean to become entrenched in an unpleasant situation.

Problems had been stacking up for months, leaving the company bemired in legal issues.

~

Bestir: The verb to bestir has been in English since AD 900. The root is in the Old English word *bestyren*, which meant to pile up wood, presumably for a fire. To bestir means to rouse from inactivity, as in to wake up. The link to woodpiles is probably related to the practice of stoking up a fire that may have dwindled or gone out while the householders were sleeping.

Coleridge was famously bestirred from his opium dreams of Kubla Khan *by an unknown man from Porlock.*

~

Bewail: People have been bewailing things in English since the twelfth century. Usually an expression of grief or loss or a lament, by the eighteenth century the word began to take on a slightly negative connotation of moaning continually or in an exaggerated fashion.

He was prone to bewailing his poor health despite doing nothing to remedy the situation.

~

Bibliobibuli: Bibliobibuli was first coined by the American satirist H. L. Mencken in the 1950s to describe a person who reads too much. It is a hybrid of the Greek word for books (*'biblio'*) and the Latin word *bibulus*, meaning to drink (or be drunk).

Being something of a bibliobibuli, at parties he liked to show off how well read he was.

~

Bifurcate: Derived from medieval Latin, *bifurcatus*, bifurcate means to split something into two forks or branches (*furca* being the Latin word for fork).

The road bifurcates before joining the motorway.

~

Bilious: Bilious has a strictly medical definition, which relates to bile and/or liver dysfunction. Medicine in the classical age believed that temperament and behaviour were determined by the four bodily humours of black bile, yellow bile, phlegm and blood (see also Phlegmatic). The adjective also has a more generalized sense of something that is particularly unpleasant, aggressive and ill-natured.

The bilious reviews by critics caused the play to close after just eight performances.

~

Blithe: A blithe person is someone who is happy and carefree. Blithe is not always a positive adjective, however, and can be used negatively to describe a lack of concern or due care and attention.

Many cycle couriers demonstrate a blithe attitude to basic road safety.

~

Bludge: The verb to bludge means to deliberately avoid work or duty and responsibility.

After a weekend of partying he decided to bludge work and spend the day on the beach instead.

~

Bodkin: From the Middle English word *bodekin* (at some point the 'e' disappeared in the spelling), a bodkin was both a needle-like instrument and a type of arrowhead. Modern bodkins are ornamental hairpins. A common punishment in the Middle Ages for insulting a vicar or priest was to have a bodkin pushed through the tongue.

All my grandmother left me in her will was her collection of ornamental bodkins and hats.

~

Boniface and Bountiful: The word boniface derives from the name of the jovial innkeeper in George Farquhar's 1707 play *The Beaux' Stratagem* – a popular comedy of the Restoration era. Used to describe a proprietor of a hotel, pub or restaurant, the term remained popular up until the mid-nineteenth century, when it began to decline. However, modern concerns of political correctness and gender-neutral labelling have led to a recent resurgence in usage, particularly in somewhat pompous restaurant reviews in newspapers and magazines. Farquhar's play made more than one contribution to the English language. The surname of the character Lady Bountiful means abundant and plentiful, but also has a secondary meaning of being a generous philanthropist.

The restaurant has recently been acquired by a new boniface with a lofty reputation for fine dining.

She was known for her bountiful gestures towards local charities.

∿

Boorish: We tend to think of boorish as describing loud, unruly, rude and insensitive behaviour. The word derives from the Old English word *būan*, which was the word for an uncivilized, country-dwelling peasant. The word is also closely linked to the Dutch word *Boer*, which means farmer. Strictly speaking, when describing someone as boorish we are saying they are behaving like a farmer, which seems a little harsh on farmers.

The boorish behaviour of professional soccer players regularly fills up column inches in the newspapers.

∿

Bounteous: Bounteous is an extension of the old Anglo-French word *bontive*, meaning a kind and generous person. The meaning has stayed more or less the same since the fifteenth century, as it still relates to giving freely and without inhibition, but it also often means an abundance of something.

Ever the bounteous hosts, they liked to throw lavish parties.

∿

Bravura: Bravura is a direct borrowing from Italian, where the word originally meant bravery, but is now more commonly used to mean a skill. The word has only been prevalent in English since the 1920s, when it was commonly used to describe stage performances (theatre, opera, ballet etc.) that were dazzling in their technical skill and execution.

A bravura performance from the prima ballerina provoked several curtain calls and a standing ovation from the audience.

∿

Brobdingnagian: In Jonathan Swift's satirical novel *Gulliver's Travels* (1726), Brobdingnag is the land of the giants that Gulliver encounters on his journeys. In short, then, anything Brobdingnagian is characterized by extraordinary size and scope. The word came into use in English soon after the publication of Swift's masterpiece, such was the popularity of the novel.

Gulliver's travels also gave rise to the adjective Lilliputian around the same time.

Building the Great Pyramids of Giza was a task of Brobdingnagian proportions for the Ancient Egyptians.

❧

Brumal: Something brumal is indicative of or occurs during the winter and often, naturally, relates to seasonal changes in the weather.

The brumal blasts of cold damp air really troubled his asthma.

❧

Bucolic: Bucolic comes from the Greek word *boukolikos* meaning a herd of cows. The word first appeared in English in the eighteenth century and was often used to describe a particular type of pastoral idyll represented in poetry and painting. The word is sometimes employed in relation to shepherds or farmers and anything with a rustic or untainted appeal.

We drove through the hills, passing through several picturesque, bucolic villages.

❧

Bumptious: An odd word of uncertain origin which first appears in English from the early nineteenth century. Charles Dickens coined the word to mean conceitedly self-assured but over time the meaning has changed to mean somebody who is loud and brash in social situations with little self-knowledge of the effects their behaviour is having upon other people in their company.

He loudly expounded his bumptious opinions and ideas.

❧

Bunkum: An insincere and/or foolish and incoherent argument. In 1820 Felix Walker, who represented Buncombe County, North Carolina, in the US House of Representatives, was determined that his voice be heard on his constituents' behalf, even though the matter up for debate was irrelevant to Walker's district and he had little to contribute. To the exasperation of his colleagues, Walker insisted on delivering a long and wearisome 'speech for Buncombe'. His persistent if insignificant harangue made buncombe (later respelled bunkum) a synonym for meaningless political claptrap and later for any kind of nonsense.

I believe the honourable gentleman's argument to be utter bunkum.

Burnish: To burnish something is to polish it in order to make it lustrous and shiny. The word derives from the Old French verb *brunir*, which meant to make something brown, and possibly derives from blacksmiths rubbing dark ointments on metals to polish them. The word can also be used, slightly disparagingly, in relation to somebody aggressively promoting their standing or reputation.

Once promoted to the next level, he tried to burnish his reputation by working long hours.

C

Cache: Cache is a hiding place or storage area. Traditionally somewhere to squirrel away provisions or items that need to be kept somewhere safe, in the modern age cache is also a computing word relating to the part of a computer's memory where temporary files are stored.

Several houses were raided by security services, who found a cache of weapons and explosives.

Cachexia: The word cachexia has existed in English since the sixteenth century and is the name given to wasting diseases and malnutrition, generally associated with any number of chronic diseases but most commonly with the brutal effects of starvation.

The word derives from the Greek word *kachexia*, meaning to be in a bad condition.

Cachexia is an inevitable consequence of terminal cancer.

∼

Cachinnate: Given its closeness in spelling to cachexia and cache, it would be reasonable to assume that the verb to cachinnate involves something furtive or unpleasant. Quite the opposite in fact – to cachinnate is to let out a loud and raucous, uncontrollable bout of laughter. The word derives from the Latin for loud laughter, *cachinnare*.

I cachinnated so long and loudly at the circus clowns I thought my sides would split.

∼

Cadaverous: The appearance or qualities of a human corpse is a clear definition of cadaverous. However, the word is also used, often quite negatively, to describe people who are excessively thin, pallid and grey in appearance or lifeless in character.

He spent an hour in a tedious meeting, the cadaverous head accountant going over the monthly figures.

∼

Cadence: Cadence, deriving from the Latin verb *cadere*, meaning to fall, was first used by English speakers in the fourteenth century and usually refers to a rhythmic sequence or flow of sounds in language or music, though it can pertain to the sounds of nature, e.g. bird calls. Cadence is most familiarly used when referring to the way a particular person speaks or, more recently, to the rhythms used by rap artists, but can also be used in a military context when referring to the rhythmic chants sung by soldiers to help them to keep in step.

She speaks with a soft Irish cadence.

∼

Cadge: The verb to cadge derives from a Middle English word *cadgear*, meaning a travelling salesman who toured rural areas selling goods and produce. Over time this gave rise to the verb to cadge, which originally meant to carry or transport something but by the 1800s had developed the negative connotation of to acquire something for free either by begging or persuasion.

Even though he doesn't smoke he always tries to cadge cigarettes.

～

Caducity: Caducity will happen to us all, in varying degrees, one day, so it's not much comfort to know an unusual word for the condition. The word developed from the French word *caduc*, meaning null and void or the transitory process of something becoming obsolete. The word has come to be used as a synonym for senility and dementia and the decline of cognitive faculties in the brain.

Regular loss of short-term memory is a symptom of developing caducity.

～

Cajole: Cajole is derived from the French word *cajoler*, meaning to urge or coax someone into doing something, usually after meeting some resistance. The word may also have stemmed from the Anglo-French word *cage* and so suggests that it is a process of trapping somebody into a certain situation.

They had to be cajoled into doing their homework with the offer of treats and rewards.

～

Callipygian: *Kalli* is a girl's name of Greek origin that translates as 'the fairest and most beautiful'. *Pygē* is the Greek word for our backside. In English, therefore, to be described as callipygian is to be in possession of a pair of beautifully shaped buttocks.

Beyoncé is renowned for her callipygian figure.

～

Callow: Callowness of youth is an expression denoting inexperience, immaturity and innocence. The word callow has a peculiar derivation, however, as it is descended from the Old English word *calu*, meaning bald. By the Middle English period, *calu* no longer meant loss of hair but lack of feathers, particularly in relation to newly born birds that were unable to fly. Hence eventually the word developed into an adjective to describe youthful naïveté.

I was approached by a callow youth who seemed lost and agitated.

∼

Calumniate: To calumniate is to besmirch a reputation by making false statements or by making malicious accusations.

Part of John Adams' short-lived and controversial Seditions Act passed by Congress in 1798 briefly made it illegal to calumniate the US president.

∼

Candour: Candour traces back to the Latin verb *candēre*, meaning to shine or glow. Candour is often used in relation to language that expresses openness, fairness and honesty.

He spoke with refreshing candour about the problems his family had endured.

∼

Capacious: Something 'capable' of containing or storing a great deal.

The capacious museums on Berlin's Museum Island contain thousands of fascinating artefacts.

∼

Capricious: A capricious person is someone who is impulsive and unpredictable. The word is often used to describe the weather in countries where it can be notoriously volatile or erratic.

The recent capricious weather in the Caribbean has put off many tourists from travelling there.

∼

Captious: A captious argument is one delivered with the sole intention of entrapping or confusing. A captious person is somebody marked by a disposition to find faults and deliver quibbling criticisms. Both words are closely linked to the Latin verb *capere*, meaning to take, which also provides the stem for the words capture and captivate.

The professor's seminars were captious affairs on account of his tendency to play devil's advocate and bombard his students with unfathomable questions.

❧

Carouse: A carouse can be jolly good fun indeed, as it involves excessive and unhindered drinking of alcohol. As a verb, although rarely used, to carouse is to propose a toast after which everyone is required to empty their glasses. A carouser is somebody who enjoys both of the above.

We went out to carouse around the local bars and clubs.

❧

Catachresis: Catachresis is a word beloved of grammarians, particularly those of a prescriptivist persuasion. On a basic level, catachresis means the misuse of words in a particular context. It is sometimes used in the context of paradoxical phrases, so is close in meaning to an oxymoron. Catachresis is often used by poets as a deliberate stylistic effect, as illustrated below.

That she might mow the beard, shave the grass, pin the plank, or nail my sleeve.

Alexander Pope, *Peri Bathous, or The Art of Sinking in Poetry* (1727)

❧

Cephalic: Cephalic relates to anything to do with the head, such as physical measurements and appearance. Demons and goats have cephalic horns, for example, and infants' cephalic measurements are often taken in childhood.

When the alien finally appeared on screen the audience gasped at its cephalic tentacles.

∼

Cerebral: In a previous incarnation as the Latin word *cerebrum*, cerebral has been in English-language medical terminology for the brain since the 1600s. The adjective is a direct borrowing from the French *cérébrale*, meaning intellectually stimulating, which didn't appear in English until the early nineteenth century. The generalized meaning, therefore, is something more likely to excite the mind than rouse the emotions.

The cerebral plays of Samuel Beckett are not to everyone's taste.

∼

Chasten: This derives from the Latin verb *castigare*, meaning to punish (the word castigate has the same root). Over time, however, more people have felt chastened by a humiliating experience than have actively chosen to chasten someone. For the latter, we simply verbally castigate instead.

The players looked thoroughly chastened by the boos from the crowd after another heavy defeat.

∼

Chryselephantine: Chryselephantine describes something made from or adorned with gold and ivory. The Ancient Greeks were very fond of coating the statues of the gods in rare and precious materials, so it is no surprise that the word derives directly from the Greek *chryselephantinos* (there is an elephant in there somewhere if you look carefully).

The National Archeological Museum of Athens contains numerous examples of lavish, chryselephantine art.

∼

Chthonic: Derived from the Greek word *chthon*, meaning the earth, anything chthonic (or less commonly chthonian) relates to what lies beneath the earth. Ancient Greek mythology is full of tales of the underworld, of its rulers Hades and Persephone, the chthonic gods of the subterranean realm. The word occasionally pops up in slightly pretentious descriptions of crime lords and secret terrorist organizations.

The Freemasons are a chthonic organization, their dealings and actions shrouded in secrecy.

~

Cibarious: From the Latin *cibus* (food) – anything relating to food, or edible food at least, can be called cibarious.

The domestic goddess has once again delighted us with her cibarious offerings.

~

Clemency: A word mostly used in legal terminology – to plea for clemency is to ask for a lighter punishment than someone probably deserves (or due to mitigating circumstances). The word derives from the Latin word *clemens* (or clement), meaning mild or calm. Interestingly, weather forecasters often talk of inclement weather – weather that will be neither mild, nor calm.

The plea for clemency to the judge fell on deaf ears.

~

Cogent: The Latin word *cogere* means to drive something or bind something together. Originally, the word cogent related to power and influence over something or someone – the power to drive things forward. In modern usage, cogent is used to describe pertinent and well-constructed ideas or arguments.

The minister's arguments for providing tax cuts for corporations were far from cogent.

~

Cognoscente: A direct borrowing from the Italian word *cognoscente* (although modern Italian curiously spells the word *conoscente* these days), this means to know or have knowledge of. Cognoscente is often used in fairly disparaging terms to describe someone with highbrow tastes and pompous opinions on art, food, football, whatever …

There is a general feeling that opera is only for the cognoscente and the wealthy individual.

~

Commensurate: Derived from the Latin noun *mensura*, meaning measure, commensurate is something that is corresponding in size, extent, amount or degree.

The salary was roughly commensurate for someone of her age and ability.

~

Complacent versus Complaisant: The homophones complacent and complaisant mean very different things. A complacent person is lacklustre in action, often with an air of self-satisfaction. A complaisant person, on the other hand, is quite the opposite and is overly willing to please, often to their own detriment.

The new secretary was very complacent, so the boss sacked her after a week.

The new secretary was very complaisant, rushing around everywhere, eager to make a good impression.

~

Conciliate: The verb to conciliate means to make two opposing positions compatible, or to appease, usually by acts of goodwill. Conciliate derives from the Latin word *conciliare*, which means to assemble or unite and persuade. *Conciliare* also provides the root for council, suggesting that the role of a council is to conciliate rival interests and parties.

The proposed changes to working conditions caused the government to attempt to conciliate the views of the unions and the management.

~

Contrite: To be contrite is to show sorrow or remorse for a wrong-doing in the hope of forgiveness. The word derives from the Latin verb *conterere*, meaning to bruise or wound. The question is then, having bruised somebody through bad behaviour and subsequently feeling bad (or bruised) about it, does that make us contrite or the victim contrite?

Although he gave a full, frank and contrite apology, I refused to accept it.

~

Corpulent: This word means to be overweight and bulky of frame. At one time, being corpulent was considered to be a sign of a person's wealth and good health.

Queen Anne is supposed to have been so corpulent by her mid-forties that she could no longer indulge her love of horse-riding.

~

Corroborate: Although most commonly used in a legal context, to corroborate means to strengthen and confirm something with evidence or a statement. It can therefore be used to back up any opinion or idea and is not just used in a court of law.

Your opinion of human nature does not corroborate my own experiences.

~

Countenance: As a noun, countenance is the expression on somebody's face, particularly an expression that displays or indicates prevailing moods or emotions. As a verb, to countenance is to give approval or to accept a specific situation or idea.

All the photographs of my father show his sombre countenance.

~

Crackerjack: The adjective crack, meaning expert, dates from the 1800s and was often applied to firearms and this to a person who was a crack shot. By the 1900s crackerjack came to describe anything marked by excellence or expertise.

He was a crackerjack at poker, often winning large pots of money in tournaments.

~

Crapulent: To be crapulent is to suffer from the ill effects of excessive eating and drinking.

He decided to do a detox in January to counteract a crapulent holiday period.

∾

Credulity: The ability or readiness to believe in something or someone, often in the face of limited proof or evidence.

Her excuses often stretched any sense of credulity to breaking point.

∾

Crepitate: To crepitate (from the Latin *crepitare*, meaning creaking) is to make a crunching or cracking sound by rubbing two related parts together. In medical terms it is often used to describe the creaking noises produced in joints of bones, for example the cracking of knuckles. The noun form crepitation is often used in relation to animals and insects.

The crepitations of the crickets kept him awake all night.

∾

Crestfallen: Crestfallen, first used in English in the late sixteenth century, describes a feeling of dejection, shame or humiliation – a *crest* being a peak, highpoint, or the plumage worn on a knight's helmet.

The actor was totally crestfallen on hearing the news that he had failed the audition.

∾

Crystalline: Crystalline relates to anything composed of, or resembling crystals. In a more generalized sense, crystalline has come to be used to describe anything that is strikingly clear or sparkling, regardless of whether it is made of crystals.

The crystalline blue waters shimmered in the sunlight.

∾

Cursory: We are all so busy these days it's no wonder we are all guilty of cursory actions – brief to the point of being superficial or possibly negligent.

Bored by her blind date, she gave only a cursory glance at the menu as she was sure she wouldn't be staying long enough to eat.

~

Custodian: Custodian is a word that highlights the subtle difference in meaning between certain words in British English and North American English. In British English a custodian cares for and protects something; however, it often has a pejorative sense of somebody who has become self-important through their duties. In North American English a custodian is a caretaker or night porter.

In the eighteenth century a small group of academics assumed the role of custodians of the rules of English grammar.

D

~

Dacoit: A dacoit is a member of a criminal gang, principally in India, Pakistan and Burma. The word came into English via Hindustani and is an Anglicization of the word for bandit.

The mountains of Pakistan are plagued by roving gangs of dacoits.

~

Dactyl: A term used in poetry to describe a metre consisting of one long and two short syllables or of one stressed and two unstressed syllables. Words such as basketball or tenderly are dactylic words. Dactyl comes from the Middle English word *dactile* via the Greek word *daktylos*, meaning finger.

Alfred Lord Tennyson was fond of writing poetry in dactylic metre.

~

Daedal: Daedalus was the architect in Greek mythology who designed the labyrinth in Crete to house the beastly Minotaur. *Daedalus* in Latin and Greek means skilfully composed or constructed, hence anything daedal (or daedalean) is intricate, clever and complex.

He opened the back of the computer and was confronted by a daedal mesh of wires and circuits.

Dagoba: A dagoba is a sacred shrine for storing spiritual relics in the Far East. The word is a strange mix of different Far Eastern languages, with traces of Singhalese, Pali and Sanskrit (Hindi). George Lucas borrowed the word for the name of the planet that was home to the Jedi-Master (and spiritual guru of the force) Yoda.

The Ruwanwelisaya Dagoba is a must-see highlight for tourists in Sri Lanka.

Dander: A curious word of uncertain origin, dander can mean either dandruff or temper and rage. Various theories have been proposed as to where the word derives its angry connotations, from tearing one's hair out (and thereby causing dandruff) to the more likely derivation from the Dutch phrase *op donderen*, which means to explode in a fit of rage.

Sunday drivers really get my dander up when I need to get somewhere in a hurry.

Dandiprat: A dandiprat was originally a small sixteenth-century coin. Over time (once the coin had gone out of circulation) the word came to mean a small, insignificant person of questionable hygiene and appearance, such as a street urchin or somebody with a childish character.

In Dickens' Oliver Twist*, Fagin rules over a gang of thieving dandiprats.*

Dastard and Dastardly: Dastard is a Middle English word from which the adjective dastardly, meaning wicked and cruel, derives. A dastard, although treacherous and untrustworthy, was essentially a coward, too. Dastardly has a sense of being irredeemably rotten and evil.

Harry Flashman is the dastardly anti-hero of George MacDonald Fraser's popular historical novels.

∼

Debacle: In its original uses, debacle (from the French word *débâcle*) meant the breaking up of ice, such as a frozen lake or river, and/or the rush of ice or water that follows such an action. This eventually led to debacle also being used to mean a violent and destructive flood. Over time this usage broadened to describe anything that went disastrously wrong or not according to plan.

The wedding was a total debacle from start to finish.

∼

Debauch: To debauch has an archaic meaning of persuading somebody to be disloyal or traitorous. This developed into the noun debaucher, a person intent on leading others away from a life of virtue or chastity. In modern times, the adjective debauched is most commonly used to describe a person living a morally slack or hedonistic lifestyle.

He opened several bottles of champagne in an effort to debauch his somewhat circumspect guests.

∼

Debilitate versus Enfeeble: Derived from the Latin *debilitare*, meaning to weaken, debilitate has various close synonyms such as enfeeble. Although closely related in sense, the two words have different Latin roots. As a general rule debilitate tends to be used in medical contexts, such as suffering from a debilitating condition. To enfeeble can be used in wider contexts and situations.

Parkinson's disease is a debilitating condition.

The government has become enfeebled by a lack of leadership.

∼

Decadent: To be decadent means to decay; the word is intrinsically linked to the fall of the Roman Empire and the historical moral decay of its ruling class. The word has developed a sense of unabashed hedonism and indulgence of sensual pleasure.

Advertising, however, has adopted the word to describe things that are rich and overtly luxurious.

We went for high tea in The Grand Hotel and indulged in a decadent spread of cakes and pastries.

~

Deciduous: Deciduous is primarily a botanical term relating to plants and trees that shed their leaves either seasonally or at certain points in their life cycle. The word comes from the Latin *decidere*, meaning to fall off. Deciduous is occasionally used in a figurative sense to describe something ephemeral, i.e. short-lived.

It would have been a perfect afternoon if the deciduous sunshine had lingered a little longer.

~

Declaim: Declaim derives from the Latin *declamare*, meaning to cry out. When we declaim, however, we are directing our words at an audience, just like an actor on a stage or a politician on a podium. To declaim one's thoughts in polite company is not always a good idea.

Shakespeare's words have more resonance when declaimed by an actor on stage than when read off the page.

~

Declension: In linguistics, declension is the inflection (changing the form of a word) of nouns, pronouns, adjectives to indicate certain aspects such as number, gender or case. As illustrated in the example below, Shakespeare, however, coined a new meaning of the word in his play *Richard III*, using the word to denote something suddenly deteriorating, in this case the reputation of a courtier after committing adultery.

A beauty-waning and distressèd widow,
Even in the afternoon of her best days,
Made prize and purchase of his wanton eye,
Seduced the pitch and height of his degree
To base declension and loathed bigamy.

William Shakespeare, *Richard III*, Act 3, Scene 1

≈

Declivity: *Clivus* is the Latin word for slope, so with the prefix *de* we have a downward slope. The word is often used in a figurative sense to describe a slump or downward trend, such as in economic performance. The antonym of declivity is acclivity, meaning an upward slope.

Stocks and shares have suffered a marked declivity in value since the start of the year.

≈

Defalcation: Defalcation has always had a relationship with money. Originally the word was used to describe a general reduction or loss, such as a defalcation in profits causing a defalcation in wages. By the nineteenth century, the term had come to its modern meaning of the act of embezzlement and fraud. Perhaps someone suddenly realized what was causing a marked loss in revenue.

The two directors were arrested and charged with the defalcation of company profits.

≈

Defenestrate: To defenestrate is to throw something out of a window. The word derives from the Latin *fenestra*, meaning window. The word is often used figuratively to describe the act of removing somebody from a position of power and authority. The origins of this lie in an infamous historical incident in Prague Castle in 1618 that led in part to the Thirty Years War. In 1617 Roman Catholic officials in Bohemia – in violation of the guarantees of religious liberty laid down in the Letter of Majesty (Majestätsbrief) of Emperor Rudolf II (1609) – closed Protestant chapels that were being constructed by citizens of the towns of Broumov and Hrob. Two local politicians were tried by an assembly and found guilty of defying the Emperor's edict, and as punishment they were thrown out of one of the battlement windows of Prague Castle. The two men fell some eighty metres but remarkably suffered only minor injuries – a fact that local Catholics were quick to claim as a miracle.

I was enraged by the inanity of so many television programmes that I defenestrated my TV set.

~

Defray: To defray is to provide a payment for something or to cover the financial burden a situation has engendered. It is an oddly archaic word that derives from the Middle French *deffroyer*, meaning to expend.

The sale of advertising space in the magazine was able to defray the costs of publication.

~

Deglutition: Deglutition is a rarely used word to describe the act of swallowing. Derived directly from the French word *déglutition*, it is related to another English word, glutton (someone who eats excessively and quickly).

The soreness in her throat made deglutition very painful.

~

Degust: The instance of tasting, especially a series of small portions. Derived from the French *dégustation*, from *de-* + *gustare*, meaning to taste.

The degustation menu at the newly opened restaurant gave the chef an opportunity to demonstrate the full range of his talents.

~

Dehortation: A dehortation is a strong argument or piece of advice against a particular course of action. It is most commonly used in legal jargon. The word is rarely used but is the antonym of exhortation, the difference being that dehortation is to dissuade whereas exhortation is to persuade.

Nobody thought that the couple would be suited to marriage but not a single person offered any dehortation at the time.

~

Deleterious: Derived from the Greek word *dēlētērios*, meaning to hurt, something deleterious is harmful, often to one's health.

The deleterious effects of smoking are well documented.

~

Deliquesce: Deliquesce means to dissolve or melt into liquid and is often used in botany to describe plants becoming rotten and turning to mush. Derived from the Latin *deliquescere*, meaning to be fluid, a more elegant and figurative use is to describe the act of slowly melting, fading or dissolving away.

He lay roasting in the sun, deliquescing in the extreme heat.

~

Delitescent: Something that is delitescent is hidden away, often furtively. The term is derived from the Latin verb *delitescere*, meaning to hide.

It is the delitescent nature of the civil service that means Whitehall officials rarely address the media.

~

Delusion versus Delusive: The noun delusion means a false belief in something, often in opposition to evidence to the contrary. Delusion relates to people, whereas the adjective delusive relates to a quality that deceives, such as ideas or appearances.

He had clear delusions of grandeur.

Modern television advertising promotes the delusive idea that material objects bring happiness.

~

Demarcate and Demarcation: In 1493, a Spanish noun, *demarcación*, was used to name the new meridian dividing Spain and Portugal, and the New World territory between South and Central America. This sense of marking something filtered into English as the noun demarcation and the verb to demarcate, meaning to set the limits of something.

The boundaries between what is acceptable and unacceptable regarding the treatment of women were not clearly demarcated in official policy.

~

Demur: Originally, to demur meant to hesitate or delay something, the word deriving from the Middle English word *demuren*, meaning to linger. The modern usage of demur is to object to something or counteract with an action.

It seemed inevitable that the union would demur over the pay deal and call a strike.

～

Dendriform: Dendriform or dendrific is a description given to an object that is tree-like in appearance or manner.

The dendriform structures in the park were Gaudí's tribute to the wonders of nature.

～

Dendrochronology: Dendrochronology is a botanical term for the scientific method of determining the age of a tree by counting the rings on a cross-section of the trunk.

In Muir Wood in California there is a fallen Giant Sequoia on which a dendrochronological timeline has been carved showing major historical events of the last two thousand years.

～

Denizen: Derived from the Middle English word *denizeine*, meaning inhabitant or dweller, denizen is rarely used to describe people from a particular place (its original meaning) but rather denotes people from a particular class or social set.

The denizens of New York's nightclubs embraced the disco craze in the later 1970s.

～

Denude: From the Latin word *nudus*, meaning naked (nude). To denude something, naturally enough, is to strip it bare of its surface covering. The word is often used in botany to describe stripping bark from trees or clearing plants from an area of land.

Environmental campaigners continue to lobby against the denuding of the rainforests.

～

Deprecate: The Latin verb *deprecatus* provides the root for deprecate. Although it originally meant to attempt to avert a looming catastrophe by prayer, in modern secular times this meaning has been abandoned in favour of deprecate being closely related to depreciate. To deprecate is to either talk something down or belittle.

A modest man, he deprecated his contribution to the local charity.

～

Depute: Derived from the Anglo-French *deputer*, meaning to assign, to depute is to delegate an action or responsibility to somebody else.

Security officers have been deputed to guard the main entrance to the building.

～

Deracinate: The word deracinate entered English from the Middle French word *desraciner*, meaning to uproot. Originally, the word referred simply to pulling up plants by the root. Over time, however, deracinate developed a metaphorical meaning relating to removing cultural and ethical influences from people or groups.

One major problem working-class students encounter at elite universities is a sense of being deracinated from their background.

～

Desiccated: Something that is dried up is desiccated, a word that comes from the Latin *siccus* (dry). Just about anything deprived of moisture becomes desiccated, from fruit and foodstuffs to arid landscapes and corpses. Desiccated is also occasionally used in a figurative sense to describe someone or something deprived of emotional vitality.

His pared-down, desiccated, prose style was a marked departure from his previous novels.

The skin of the desiccated mummy looked like old paper.

～

Desultory: In the circus games of Ancient Greece and Rome, a desultor was a performer who leapt from the backs of galloping horses (sometimes as many as six at a time) to entertain the crowd. It is from this acrobatic feat that the word desultory derives. A desultory argument is one which leaps from point to point, seemingly without any focus or structure. Likewise, desultory performances by sports teams are ones marked by a lack of concentration or application.

The coach was fired by the general manager after a season of desultory performances on the field.

∼

Detrude: To detrude is to thrust or force downwards. The word has its root in the Latin *trūdere*, meaning thrust, with the downward prefix *de* added to it.

The government must take radical action to detrude the rising cost of living.

∼

Dichotomy: Traditionally a dichotomy was something that could be divided into two distinct groups or concepts that are contradictory or opposing, such as heaven and hell. This has led to the idea of dichotomy meaning two things that are opposed to each other, such as the dichotomy between communism and capitalism.

The essay discussed the dichotomy between good and evil in modern gothic fiction.

∼

Didactic: Derived from *didaktikos*, a Greek word that means apt at teaching, and first entering the English language in the seventeenth century, didactic means to teach and instruct as well as being artistic. Parables are often described as being didactic, as there is a moral to be learned from the story. However, in recent years the word has sometimes come to be used in a derogatory manner for a piece that is overly instructive, pompous or dull.

The students were losing concentration during the lecture due to its overly didactic style.

～

Diffident: The Latin verb *fidere*, meaning to trust, is responsible for several words in English (confident, fidelity and fiduciary). The original meaning of diffident was untrustworthy but over time it has developed in relation to personality traits. A diffident person is shy, quiet and modest, perhaps through lack of confidence (or, literally, self-trust). Confident is the antonym of diffident and means having self-trust.

Although renowned for her extravagant stage performances, the singer was actually quiet and diffident in social circles.

～

Dilapidate: Originally dilapidate meant to squander something. It derives from the Latin verb *dilapidare*, meaning to destroy something by pelting it with stones. In the modern sense, dilapidate retains a sense of impending destruction but more through neglect and misuse.

Our garden shed is very dilapidated and should be pulled down.

～

Diminutive: Diminutives in grammatical terms indicate smallness through the use of affixes to base words. As an adjective, diminutive also describes smallness, sometimes in a positive and sometimes in a derogatory way.

The diminutive batsman put in a sterling performance.

Kitchenette is the diminutive of kitchen.

～

Dishevelled: Dishevelled is derived from the Old French word for hair (*chevel*). Although often used to describe people of scruffy, unkempt appearance, strictly speaking dishevelled should be applied to anyone having a bad hair day.

The politician's wilfully dishevelled appearance was in evidence at the press conference.

~

Disinterested versus Uninterested: A common solecism, people often say they are disinterested when they are bored or don't really care. The word means to take up a position of impartiality, as an observer who has no stake in whatever is being disputed or discussed. An uninterested person simply wouldn't bother.

I was invited to the conference to act as a disinterested observer.

I was invited to the conference but was uninterested in the subject matter so I declined.

~

Disputatious: An extension of the noun/verb dispute, disputatious relates to persons or groups with a vested interest or fondness for starting and conducting arguments.

To be an effective lawyer it helps to cultivate a disputatious personality.

~

Dissemble: The Middle English word *dissymblen* derives from the Latin *dissimulare*, meaning to conceal, and gives us the graceful but furtive verb dissemble. When we wilfully obscure information, or we fake or pretend, we dissemble.

She dissembled her intentions to sell her mother's house from the rest of the family.

~

Dissimilate: To dissimilate is to change a sound or sounds in a word to another when the word originally had adjacent sounds. This occurs with homonyms, where how the word is pronounced changes the meaning.

The letter 'r' in the final syllable of French marbre *is dissimilated to 'l' in its English form marble.*

~

Dissolute: Dissolute is often used to describe a person who frequently gets drunk and/or who lives a lifestyle devoted to morally suspect behaviour or hedonistic pursuits.

In the favelas of Brazil it is hard not to notice the dissolute and degrading aspects of human nature.

~

Dithyramb(ic): Originally, a dithyramb was a wild poem sung or chanted on feast days in Ancient Greece for the god Dionysus (*Dithrambos*). The adjective dithyrambic in English has come to mean any piece of speech or writing that is excessive and over the top in its praise, and frankly rather foolish.

The father of the bride gave a dithyrambic speech about his daughter's virtues on her wedding day.

~

Dolorous: Derived from the Old French word *dolerous*, meaning painful, dolorous is used in relation to sadness and matters of the heart in poetic and melancholy contexts.

She gazed out of the window, her dolorous heart weighing heavy in her breast.

~

Dotard: The Middle English word *dotus* (from the thirteenth century), meaning to dote over, quickly became an insult in Shakespeare's times for a doddering old fool. It is basically defined as someone in their advancing years or dotage.

'Away with the dotard; to the jail with him!'

William Shakespeare, *The Taming of the Shrew*, Act 5, Scene 1

~

Doughty: One of the few words that has survived relatively unscathed from Old English, doughty comes from *dohtig*, meaning to have strength and worthiness. A doughty person is someone who doesn't give up but perseveres.

*Doughty and resolute, the Russians held firm during the siege of
Leningrad.*

≈

Doyen: In French, *doyen* means dean – the most respected member
of a group. Originally, the word related to somebody in the military
who was put in charge of ten soldiers or more. In English it means
somebody renowned for their expertise in a particular field or
occupation.

*Sir Anthony Hopkins is regarded as a doyen of the British acting
profession.*

≈

Draconian: Draconian comes from Draco, the name of a seventh-
century BC Athenian legislator. He created a code of legislation
which was notable for its severity; even minor offences were
punishable by death, and failure to pay one's debts could result in
slavery. Therefore, draconian came to mean a consequence that was
overly harsh, e.g. an excessive fine for dropping litter.

*It was generally thought that the magistrates had been rather
draconian when deciding on the length of his driving ban.*

≈

Dubiety: A peculiar word given that it has close links to the
Latin word *dubius*, meaning doubt. Dubious in modern English
means probably not to be trusted, whereas dubiety is a feeling of
uncertainty or hesitance.

*Any sense of dubiety about the job was quickly dispelled after the
first morning in post.*

≈

Dulcet: The Latin word *dulcis* meant something that was sweet
tasting. The adjective dulcet is often used to describe the sound of a
voice. It is possible that the change between sweet tasting and sweet

sounding came to English via the Italian musical term (via Latin) *dolce*, meaning to be played (or sung) sweetly.

Her dulcet tones were very seductive.

Duplicitous: Duplicitous comes from a Latin word meaning double or twofold, and its original meaning in English is that what you are saying is not what you actually mean.

The salesman's talk was definitely duplicitous, as they found out after they bought the car.

Dystopia versus Utopia versus Orwellian: Sir Thomas More (1478–1535) introduced the word utopia into English in his philosophical novel of the same name. More's utopia was an idealized, imaginary future society or state. Curiously, the antonym 'dystopia' – a dark and forbidding state of misery and conflict – didn't appear in English until the mid-nineteenth century, when it was coined by John Stuart Mill in a speech to the House of Commons. The adjective dystopian is used to describe a genre of literature and film featuring future totalitarian societies, such as described in George Orwell's novel *1984*, which has itself given rise to the adjective Orwellian, a synonym for dystopian.

Most modern science fiction, though presenting a dystopian vision of the future, is often passing comment on the present state of civilization.

E

Earworm: Earworm is a modern word that has entered into English from the German term *Ohrwurm*, which describes a melody or song that comes into our minds randomly, unconsciously and repetitively.

That jingle is a real earworm; I've been humming it for days.

~

Easement: Easement is basically the legal right to trespass on someone else's land. For example, should you buy a house, and then somebody else buys up all the land around your house, a deed of easement needs to be negotiated in order for you to have full access to your property.

The landowner grumbled about walkers on his land in spite of the easement agreements in place.

~

Eavesdrop: The eaves of a building are the overhanging parts of the roof that cover the external walls. The eavesdrop were the drips of water dropping from the roof on to the ground below. In one of many creative uses of the English language a rather dull noun became a verb describing the activity of listening in on other people's conversations, presumably, in a figurative sense, catching drips and drops of information.

Shakespeare's plays, especially the comedies, are marred by the repetitive use of eavesdropping as a plot device.

~

Ebberman: An angling term for fishing enthusiasts who prefer to do their fishing under bridges, presumably to catch certain ebbs in the current of the river.

A skilled angler, his best competition results came when adopting an ebberman approach.

~

Ebriosity: Taken from the Latin word *ebrius*, meaning drunk, ebriosity is a rather elegant word for alcoholism.

The actor's career was ruined by his ebriosity.

~

Ebullient: Somebody described as ebullient is bubbling with excitement and anticipation. The word derives from the Latin word *ebullire*, meaning to boil or bubble. The word has existed in

English since the fifteenth century and was possibly a culinary term originally before the meaning was expanded to be used figuratively to describe human characteristics.

The team were in an ebullient mood in the dressing room before the final match of the season.

∾

Ecdemomania: One of many, spurious 'manias', relating to behavioural compulsions (e.g. pyromania, nymphomania etc.), ecdemomania is a pathological compulsion to move from place to place and never settle down – known in less self-obsessive times as being restless or having 'itchy feet'.

I think I must be an ecdemomaniac as I can't stand to stay in one place for too long.

∾

Ecdysiast: There are several 'polite' descriptions for striptease artists, ranging from burlesque artist to exotic dancer, but by far the most highfaluting is an ecdysiast. The word was first recorded in English in 1940 by the American journalist H. L. Mencken (probably satirically) and is formed by combining the Greek word *ekdysīs*, meaning to shed something, with the word enthusiasm.

Whenever people ask what I do for a living I say I'm an ecdysiast – they assume I work in the medical profession.

∾

Echolalia and Echopraxia: Echolalia is an often involuntary, pathological condition or verbal tic whereby a person repeats what is spoken to them by other people as if echoing them. Echopraxia is a similar condition but concerns involuntary repetition of another person's gestures or actions.

Although often considered a possible symptom of autism, most infants go through a stage of echolalia during language acquisition.

∾

Eclectic: Eclectic describes something composed of different elements drawn from a number of varied sources. The word comes from the Greek verb *eklektikos*, meaning to select, and was used originally to describe ancient philosophers who, rather than being committed to a single doctrine, derived their philosophy from any number of schools of thought. Its first recorded use in English was in 1683.

The diners at the new restaurant were impressed by the eclectic range of the menu.

~

Ecphrasis: An ecphrasis is a scholarly term for a literary description, criticism or extended comment on a work of visual art.

For homework please read Robert Hughes' ecphrasis on Goya's Black Paintings.

~

Edacious: Originally relating to having an extraordinarily large appetite, edacious has developed as an alternative to voracious in terms of meaning a seemingly insatiable need to consume something.

My wife has an edacious appetite for trashy television soap operas.

~

Edentate: *Edentare* in Latin means to make toothless, thus edentate means to be without teeth.

My grandmother's edentate smile used to give me the creeps.

~

Edulcorate: Originally, to edulcorate derived from the Latin verb *edulcare* (make sweet), related to sweetening food. The word can, however, be used in a general sense to describe people who may need to be 'sweetened' as a means to an end.

The lavish state banquet thrown for the president was clearly an attempt to edulcorate him before the trade summit.

~

Effete: *Effetus* in Latin means no longer fertile or fruitful and was initially used in relation to the breeding of livestock and working animals. When applied to humans it took on the meaning of being exhausted or ineffective due to age, a shorthand for phrases such as 'over the hill'. Then, in the 1920s, for reasons unknown, the term effete took on the meaning of dressing and behaving in an effeminate manner.

What do you think of my new haircut? Is it too effete?

~

Efficacious: Efficacious is used to describe something that gives the desired effect. It has been used in the English language since the beginning of the sixteenth century.

The new oven cleaner proved to be efficacious.

~

Effluvium: A direct borrowing from Latin, effluvium is something flowing out from somewhere. In modern English it has negative connotations relating to sewage, waste products and pollution.

The effluvium from untreated sewage is polluting the rivers and sea.

~

Effulgent: Anything that shines with splendour and brilliance can be described as effulgent. To effulge is to shine forth, although as a verb, effulge has never quite taken off. Both words have their root in one of the many Latin words for shine, *fulgēre*.

As if from the heavens, the clouds broke and an effulgent light shone down.

~

Effusive: The Latin verb *effundere*, meaning an outpouring, is the root for effusive – an enthusiastic, usually positive, outburst of praise and reverence for something or someone.

They offered effusive thanks for our help as volunteers.

~

Egestion: The act of dispelling waste material from an organism; most specifically, defecation.

I got caught short on the bus home and had to hold in an egestion.

∾

Eidolon and Eidolonism: In Ancient Greek literature an eidolon was a phantom image of a dead person believed to be their spirit; in short, a ghost. Eidolonism is the word for a fervent belief in ghosts and the afterlife.

I don't believe in eidolonism; if ghosts exist, why do people only ever see them at night?

∾

Eisegesis versus Exegesis: Eisegesis and exegesis are literary terms relating to the study of texts. Both words have their root in the Greek verb *exegeisthai*, meaning to explain or interpret. Originally, exegesis related to attempts by theologians to interpret the Bible and draw meanings from it relevant to their life and epoch. The word has broadened to include any literary text, particularly novels and plays. An exegesis places emphasis upon the text itself and draws conclusions by close analysis. An eisegesis is often a subjective reading based upon personal ideas and prejudices.

The professor failed my essay on Flaubert and suggested I look up the difference between exegesis and eisegesis.

∾

Ejecta: Ejecta is any substance, object or person that has been thrown out (Latin *ejectus*) from somewhere. This could be magma from a volcano, hooligans (in plural) from a nightclub or, in medical terminology, a polite term for vomit.

It is not uncommon to find the ejecta from the city's clubs and bars staggering around the streets on a Saturday night.

∾

Élan: To do something with élan is often thought of as to do it with a certain style or panache. The word is a direct borrowing from French and actually originally meant to rush or dash around frenetically. In its strictest sense in English the word means to set about a task with vigorous enthusiasm and spirit.

The street dancers performed their routines with great élan.

~

Eldritch: In Middle English *elfriche* was the word for a sort of netherworld of fairies and spirits. The adjective eldritch evolved into a description of a weird and eerie sound, particularly a voice.

'The woman, whose voice had risen to a kind of eldritch sing-song, turned with a skip, and was gone.'

Robert Louis Stevenson, *Kidnapped*

~

Elenctic: A rhetorical term relating to an aspect of a statement or argument that serves to refute an accusation or claim.

At Nuremberg several Nazi war criminals presented the elenctic argument that they were only following orders.

~

Elide: From the Latin *elidere*, meaning to strike out, to elide means to amend or omit, alter or suppress.

After a court injunction was granted, the newspapers were forced to elide the name of the celebrity at the centre of the scandal in their reportage.

~

Elinguation: The word for a rather grisly punishment in the Middle Ages, namely that of removing the tongues of criminals or heretics. The Earl of Wessex is alleged to have once tried to pass a law stating that people found guilty of slander should be punished by elinguation.

After suffering the horror of elinguation, the unfortunate victim was no longer able to speak.

~

Elysian: In classical mythology Elysium was a place of paradise for heroes immortalized by the gods. Elysian can be used to describe any place of peace and tranquillity.

The tranquil beauty of Provence invokes a sense of Elysian bliss in some travellers.

~

Emacity: From the Latin *emaciates*, meaning the desire to buy, emacity is the urge, desire or fondness for buying things, or more generally for spending money.

Whenever my mother is on holiday a compulsive emacity grips her and she ends up with a whole load of junk she neither wants nor needs.

~

Embonpoint: In Middle French the phrase *en bon point* was used to describe someone of healthy size and condition. In the nineteenth century an Anglicized version of the word begins to crop up in the works of the likes of Charlotte Brontë and George Eliot to describe women of heavy-set, yet comely appearance.

'As erect in her comely embonpoint as a statue of Ceres.'

George Eliot, *Adam Bede* (1859)

~

Embrangle: To brangle in Middle English meant to quarrel with somebody (possibly a hybrid of brawl and wrangle). By the seventeenth century, to embrangle came to act as a synonym for embroiling other people in a situation, often negatively.

He set about embrangling everyone he knew in his dubious investment opportunities.

~

Emollient: We think of emollients as dermatological products to soften our hands and hair, and that is in essence the meaning of the word. However, beyond the chemist's, anything that softens something that is harsh or abrasive can be described as an emollient.

The company brought in an arbitration service as an emollient in the increasingly bitter dispute with the unions.

～

Enchiridion: An enchiridion is a small book of advice or essential information. The original enchiridion was compiled by the Greek philosopher Epictemus (AD 55–135) and outlined the virtues of stoicism. In English an enchiridion has been used since the seventeenth century as a rather pompous word for a small instruction manual on any subject. In Greek, *enchiridion* translates as 'that which can be carried in the hand'.

The Enchiridion of Epictemus *is a minor classic of Ancient Greek philosophy.*

～

Encomium: The Greeks, as with many words in English, started encomiums in praise of their triumphant heroes and athletes. From the word *enkōmion*, meaning in celebration of, an encomium is a written tribute or speech in honour of someone's achievements.

When the English master asked me to provide an encomium for our retiring head teacher I had no idea what he was talking about.

～

Endophagy: Derived as a compound word from *endo* (from within) and *phagy* (to feed on), endophagy is a rare word for when a group of humans, due to extreme circumstance, turn to cannibalism.

The film Alive *recounts the true story of air-crash victims stranded in the remote Andes who are forced into endophagy in order to survive.*

～

Endue versus Indue versus Imbue: To endue something is to provide it with a certain quality or ability. Indue is a variant of endue and to some extent the two words are interchangeable, though indue has its roots in the Latin verb *induere*, meaning to dress up. Imbue, on the other hand, has the sense of flavouring something or introducing one thing into another to give it character.

He has always been endued with a positive outlook, encouraged by his parents.

The Christmas tree was indued with sparkling baubles.

This fine artisan gin has been imbued with a careful balance of herbs and spices.

∽

Enervate: This is a much misused word, often by people who should know better. It will not take much to find politicians or journalists talking about measures to enervate the economy, when they mean invigorate or energize. Ironically, it is probably government policy that has *enervated* the economy in the first place, so perhaps they are only half wrong. To enervate means to weaken something or someone, to drain of vitality, either mentally or physically.

Prolonged under-investment only served to enervate the economy of any power to grow.

∽

Enfranchise and Disenfranchise: The original meaning of enfranchise related to slavery and the practice of setting slaves free from their owners to be self-determined. In a general sense it is the granting of the privileges of a citizen and especially to the right of suffrage (voting in public elections). Disenfranchise denotes when a group or ruling organization denies the freedom to vote to other groups.

They disenfranchised poor people by making property ownership a requirement for registering to vote.

∽

Enjambment: Taken from the French *enjamber*, meaning to straddle, enjambment is a technical term in poetry. It denotes the running over of a line of verse or couplet into another so that the sense 'runs over' without any break in the metric structure or loss of meaning.

Philip Larkin's mature poetry makes significant use of enjambment in his longer verse compositions.

≈

Enrapture: It is wonderful to be enraptured as it means we are filled with delight and joy. The word appears in the Bible to describe the love of a husband for his wife and vice versa.

The audience were enraptured by the sound of her voice.

≈

Ephemeral: When ephemeral, from the Greek word *ephēmeros*, meaning lasting a day, first appeared in print in English in the late sixteenth century, it was a scientific term applied to short-term fevers, and later, to organisms such as insects and flowers, with a very short life. Over time the word broadened to refer to anything fleeting and short-lived, and it has a rather melancholy aspect.

He gazed at the sun going down over the sea and mused on the ephemeral nature of reality.

≈

Epiphany: The Epiphany is a Christian festival to commemorate Christ first manifesting himself to Gentiles, and in the Eastern Church it is also a commemoration of the baptism of Jesus. First used in English during the fourteenth century and deriving from the late Latin *epiphania*, the un-capitalized word is used to refer to a sudden manifestation or perception of the basic meaning of something, a sudden grasp of a situation, or an illuminating realization or discovery – colloquially, 'a light-bulb moment'.

He experienced a sense of epiphany when, after a lot of research, he finally realized who his natural father was.

≈

Equanimity: Equanimity derives from *aequus*, a Latin adjective meaning level or equal. Originally the term related to fairness and balance in judgement but it has developed the sense of general harmony displayed by someone or something.

He has the capacity for notable equanimity of thought.

∾

Equilibrist: The term for a circus performer/acrobat whose acts concern high-wire walking, rope or trapeze spectacles.

The film Man on a Wire *is the true story of an equilibrist's personal quest.*

∾

Ergophobia: Although in Latin *ergo* means therefore, in Greek it is the word for work. Ergophobia is therefore a fear of work, something most right-minded people will surely experience at some point in their life.

I haven't applied for a job for years as I suffer from ergophobia.

∾

Ersatz: *Ersatz* is the German word for substitute. The word first entered into English during the First World War when, in the trenches, other substances were 'substituted' for certain commodities in short supply. Over time the word has developed into a general term for anything that is artificial or a poor substitute for the original.

It's hard not to feel that cover versions of classic songs by contestants on television talent shows are more ersatz than a yardstick of genuine talent.

∾

Eschatology: A branch of theology concerned with the final events in the history of the world or of humankind.

There is an eschatologist who walks around the streets telling everyone he meets that the world is about to end.

∾

Eschew: When we eschew something we avoid or abstain from doing it, often as a moral or practical judgement. Interestingly, Samuel Johnson predicted in his famous dictionary of 1755 that the word eschew would soon be obsolete in English, yet it has survived in rude health.

They eschewed the formalities of meeting and greeting and got straight down to business.

~

Esoteric: First used in English around 1660 and deriving from the late Latin *esotericus*, esoteric describes something that is designed for or understood by a specific group of people and that is difficult for a layperson to understand.

Although he prided himself on being able to answer many of the questions posed on the quiz show, he had to admit that those on physics were too esoteric for him.

~

Ethereal: Ethereal originally had the meaning of something heavenly or in a realm beyond the earth. For the Ancient Greeks, the ether was the realm of the gods and immortals. Over time the adjective has developed into a description of something exuding an otherworldly quality.

The twilight bathed the church spire in an ethereal glow.

~

Eunoia: Thought to have first been coined by the Greek philosopher Aristotle, who employed the term to describe the warmness of feeling between spouses essential for a balanced and happy life. However, the Roman politician and philosopher Cicero used the word to describe benevolence and kindness. A modern interpretation is the ability to display calmness and balance in speech and thought, especially when speaking in front of an audience. It is an elegant word expressing an elegant concept, and it is also the shortest word in the English language to contain all five vowels.

The speech captivated the audience with its natural sense and feeling of eunoia.

∾

Excoriate: In the fifteenth century to excoriate meant to strip off the hide of an animal, usually to make clothing. Sometime around the seventeenth century, this sense of skinning something developed a figurative meaning of harshly criticizing someone.

He delivered an excoriating assessment of the company's affairs.

∾

Exculpate and Culpable: Exculpate was adopted in the late seventeenth century from the medieval Latin *exculpatus*, and is derived from the Latin noun *culpa*, meaning blame. To exculpate or be exculpated is therefore to be free from blame. The adjective culpable is derived from the same Latin stem and means deserving of blame or responsible for something wrong or harmful.

The city council was culpable for the disaster by not heeding warnings about inadequate flood defences.

∾

Execrable: In medieval times the Latin verb *exsecrari* meant to be cursed or damned. The word execrable, derived from this, was used to describe heinous and abominable actions worthy of ultimate denouncement and sanction. However, as fire and brimstone cursing went out of fashion, the term began to be used to describe situations or things that are atrociously bad.

The food at the all-inclusive hotel was execrable, so we ate out every night.

∾

Exemplar: An exemplar is not just an example of something; it is an ideal or perfect example.

Bette Davis was the exemplar of the Hollywood film icon.

∾

Extraneous: Extraneous derives from the Latin word *extraneus*, meaning strange. There is, however, nothing strange about the modern usage of this adjective, which refers to something on the outside which is non-essential or superfluous.

Modern electrical goods are sold in boxes characterized by layer upon layer of extraneous packaging.

~

Extrinsic: Extrinsic is something on the outside not forming part of or belonging to the nature of something, such as extrinsic markings or stains on a building caused by the weather or air pollution.

The fact that the bar belonged to your grandmother is extrinsic to its value.

~

Exult versus Exalt: To exult is to feel intense joy and jubilation, usually due to some victory or successful enterprise. To exalt is used as a verb meaning to hold someone or something in very high regard. Exalt also has the sense of being lifted into a lofty position of power or status, such as to be in the presence of exalted company.

He exulted at the news of his successful job promotion.

We must resist the tendency to exalt celebrities merely because they are famous for being famous.

F

Fabliau: A coarse, often comically vulgar, narrative verse that was popular in France in the twelfth and thirteenth centuries, and in England in the fourteenth and fifteenth centuries.

Fabliaus were the nearest medieval poetry came to pornographic literature.

~

Facundity: Denoting eloquence with words and persuasive use of language, facundity derives from the Latin word *facunditas*, meaning readiness of speech.

His facundity failed him at a vital moment and he began to stammer nervously.

~

Faineant: An archaic word derived from the French *faitnient*, meaning to do nothing. A faineant is an idler, loafer or incorrigible shirker. The word can also be used as an adjective.

The character of Skimpole in Dickens' Bleak House *is faineant in his actions and behaviour.*

~

Fait Accompli: Fait accompli was adopted into the English language in around 1845 and describes something that has been done and cannot be changed.

It was clear at the outset of the meeting that the board was not being asked to make a decision but to accept a fait accompli.

~

Fanfaronade: In Spanish, a *fanfarrón* is a boastful braggart. The word migrated into English and became the noun fanfaronade – the sound of bragging and bluster.

There was much fanfaronade from both coaches in the pre-match press conference.

~

Fantabulous: A hybrid word rich in hyperbole, fantabulous is a mix of fantastic and fabulous, which, on balance, is quite unnecessary, as either root word would suffice to describe wondrous things.

Book now to secure the fantabulous holiday of a lifetime.

~

Farceur: In medieval French the verb *farcer* meant to tell jokes. The noun farceur is closely linked to the concept of farce as a form of humorous theatrical performance. A farceur is therefore the word for an accomplished performer of farces.

The theatre troupe was comprised of three highly regarded farceurs.

~

Farouche: A word with two almost contradictory meanings, farouche derives from the Old French word *forasche*, meaning to live outside. The traditional usage was to describe somebody who was shy and awkward in groups or social situations. This sense of being an outsider developed a secondary meaning of somebody excluded due to their wild and untamed behaviour.

Trouble flared in the bar after a stand-off between two gangs of farouche travellers.

~

Fascinate versus Fasciate: The original meaning of fascinate was to be bewitched or cast under a spell. This developed into a sense of becoming very interested and enamoured with something or someone. Fasciate is a zoological term to describe distinctive bands or markings of colour on animals and insects.

In the Reptile House at the zoo were some rare species of lizard with bright fasciate markings.

~

Fasti: This is a type of descriptive calendar. Originating from Ancient Rome, a fasti listed days of the week and months, and high-lighted particular days of note such as festivals, feast days and days when legal transactions were permitted.

Around twenty fasti *have been excavated from Roman ruins.*

~

Fastidious: We think of fastidious when we think of work, or a person we know who displays an almost obsessive attention to detail when approaching a task.

He was fastidious in his appearance, spending hours in the bathroom.

～

Fathom: As a noun, a fathom is a nautical measurement of water depth equal to six feet or 1.8 metres. As a verb, however, to fathom is to try to understand something that is complex or difficult.

I can't fathom him; he says one thing and then does another.

～

Fatidic: Fatidic is closely related to the word fate, and is derived from the Latin word *fatum*, meaning that which has been spoken. A number of superstitious cultures believed that fate could be prophesied by mystics and soothsayers. Anything fatidic relates to a prophecy or prediction.

He had an almost fatidic ability to pick winners of horse races.

～

Faugh: A useful word if you want to cut down on swearing. Faugh! It is an interjection to describe contempt, disgust and general annoyance at a turn of events.

Faugh! I've lost my car keys!

～

Faux-Bonhomie, Faux Pas and Faux Naif: *Faux* in French means false and is used as a prefix for various noun phrases and adjectives that have entered into English. *Faux-bonhomie* describes a person who is falsely jovial, usually for selfish reasons, or insincere. A *faux pas* (which translates literally as 'false step') is putting your foot in it in a social situation. *Faux naif* is an adjective to describe somebody who pretends to be childlike and naïve but is, in fact, nothing of the sort.

His display of faux-bonhomie *brought to mind a smiling crocodile.*

I committed the ultimate faux pas *by asking if she was pregnant.*

The faux naif *fluttering of her eyelids might fool some people but not me.*

～

Fealty: Originally, a fealty was an oath of allegiance to a leader such as a monarch, but its meaning has widened to include principles and religions. The word is essentially a hybrid of the more commonly used terms fidelity and loyalty.

> *'Fealty is to take an oath upon a book, that he will be a faithful tenant to the King.'*
>
> Francis Bacon, *The Use of Law* (1629)

~

Febrile: Febrile is a medical term for feverish reactions to an illness or virus. Derived from the Latin word for fever, *febris*, febrile has an extended usage to describe a heightened state of emotion or excitement.

> *The speeches whipped the febrile crowd up into a frenzy.*

~

Fecund: Derived from the Latin *fecundus*, meaning fertile or fruitful, anything described as fecund is capable of producing offspring, often prolifically. The word has a secondary meaning in relation to the imagination, intellect or creative output.

> *The fecund imagination of the writer Stephen King has produced many memorable novels.*

~

Felicity: One of the greatest nouns in the English language and much underused. When Edwyn Collins, the lead singer of the 1980s Scottish alternative pop band Orange Juice sang in the song 'Felicity' he was expressing one of the meanings of the word: the quality or state of being made happy by something or someone. He was also, perhaps unintentionally, right twice, as the secondary, more highbrow meaning of felicity is having felicity with language, which means using words perfectly to express ideas, emotions and thoughts.

> *She prided herself on her exquisite felicity with language.*

~

Feuillemort: A word derived from the French term *feuille morte*, which describes the colours of dead or dying leaves in the autumn.

We marvelled at the feuillemort colours in the autumn sunshine.

~

Fidelity: The Latin verb *fidere*, meaning to trust, provides the root for both uses of the word fidelity. We think of fidelity in relationships as meaning faithfulness between partners, hence mutual trust. Fidelity is also used in describing accuracy in detail, particularly in audio and visual recording and broadcasts. How faithful or accurate the recording is determines its level of fidelity.

He believed very strongly in the bond of fidelity he accepted when he got married.

~

Fiduciary: A fiduciary arrangement is a bond of confidence or trust. Often used in relation to financial arrangements, banks have fiduciary agreements with their customers.

Board members have a fiduciary responsibility to the fund.

~

Filial: Filial is derived from the Latin words *filius*, meaning son, and *filia*, meaning daughter. In English the word (since the mid-fourteenth century) describes the relationship or bond between a parent and their offspring of either sex.

His father struggled with filial responsibilities towards his children.

~

Fillip: In its strictest sense, the verb to fillip means to make a flicking gesture with the thumb and forefinger. The word predates the more common flip or flick and, over time, has developed a figurative use to describe giving sudden stimulation to something or someone.

The sandwiches provided a fillip for the children between lunch and the evening meal.

~

Fissile: The word fissile has existed in scientific writing since the sixteenth century. Fissile derives from the Latin word *fissilis*, which means a substance or material that can be split or divided. In modern times fissile is often used in relation to nuclear fusion and the splitting of the atom to release energy. However, given its longevity in the English language, anything that can be divided can be described as fissile.

The Strange Case of Dr Jekyll and Mr Hyde *is a story of a man with a fissile personality.*

∼

Flabellate: Flabellate describes anything fan-like in appearance or arrangement. The origin of the word is uncertain, although a flabellum was a fan made of leather or parchment used in Christian religious ceremonies to swat insects away from the Eucharistic elements.

The magician spread the playing cards across the table in a flabellate aspect.

∼

Flagitious, Flagellate and Flagrant: In the fourteenth century someone who was flagitious was capable of shameful or terrible acts and the term was often applied to murderers or thieves. The word is related to the Latin word for a whip, *flagrum*. Flagellate, meaning to whip or flog, derives from the same stem, presumably because wicked people were whipped and flogged for their crimes. Flagitious can be used in relation to ideas and actions and is not exclusive to people. Also related to these words is the Latin word *flagrare*, meaning to burn or scorch, which provides the root for the adjective flagrant – a term that describes an action so obviously or deliberately opposed to what is right or proper as to appear to be a flouting of law or morality.

The flagitious actions of the invading army resulted in the mass genocide of innocent civilians.

∼

Flamboyant: Flamboyant derives from the Old French word *flambé*, meaning flame. Denoting something eye-catching and wilfully showy, flamboyant was originally used to describe architecture of a striking and intricate design. By the nineteenth century the term came to be applied to people, particularly performers, who 'lit up' the stage with their larger than life personalities. The cooking term *flambé*, which means to set something aflame, derives from the same Old French root.

The lead singer was a flamboyant performer.

~

Flapdoodle: Flapdoodle, alongside its close relatives fiddlesticks and fiddle-faddle, is of unknown origin. The word first appeared towards the end of the nineteenth century and means nonsense words, comments or observations in speech or language. The Victorians were rather fond of inventing words that mean nothing at all, as evidenced in the works of Edward Lear and Lewis Carroll.

That is the biggest load of flapdoodle I have ever heard.

~

Flaunt versus Flout: To flaunt is to be ostentatious in public with the deliberate intention of being noticed. The word is of unclear origin but may link to the Old Norse word *flana*, meaning to rush around. To flout, however, is to behave very differently and means to treat something (such as rules or regulations) with contemptuous disregard.

She liked to flout the rules of social etiquette by flaunting her larger than life personality.

~

Flavescent: Flavus was a ninth-century Germanic tribal chief and warrior who defected to the Roman Empire. His original Germanic name is unknown and scholars believe the Romans gave him the name Flavus on account of his shock of blond hair. *Flavus* is the Latin word for yellow and from this derives the adjective flavescent, meaning to turn yellow or be of yellowish colour.

The light in winter, especially in the late afternoons, bathes the whole city in a flavescent glow.

❧

Fleer: Originally a Middle English word, *fleryen* via the Norse word *flire*, meaning to giggle, to fleer at somebody or something is to scoff in a derisive manner. Although it is synonymous with sneer, the difference is that sneering involves words whereas it is possible to fleer without saying anything.

The condescending duchess gave a fleering look to her love rival and turned away.

❧

Flibbertigibbet: Flibbertigibbet now means a flighty silly person, but in the past it was used to indicate something devilish, and it was employed by both Shakespeare and Sir Walter Scott in their works. Originating from the Middle English word *flepergebet*, meaning gossip or chatterer, it is onomatopoeic, created from sounds that were intended to represent meaningless chatter.

The girl in the reality TV show was a flibbertigibbet.

❧

Flite: An archaic word, largely obsolete, that has a rich etymology dating back to Old English and earlier Saxon dialects. The word *flītan* in Old English means to cause a wrangle or strife, and to flite has a similar definition in that it means to contend or complain.

He had an irritating tendency to flite over the bill in restaurants.

❧

Foison: A foison harvest in the Middle Ages was rich and bountiful, the word foison being closely related to the Latin term *fusio*, meaning an outpouring. In some Scottish dialects the word foison is used to describe a person's physical strength and stamina.

Eat your porridge up, laddie, it'll give you plenty of foison.

❧

Footling: A footling problem is usually a trivial matter. The word can also be applied to people who are inept or incompetent at their jobs.

He had to dispense with his footling assistant after a catalogue of errors.

∼

Forbear versus Forebear: The Old English verb *forberan* meant to endure or do without. This meaning of forbear is now largely obsolete. Shakespeare used forbear to mean leaving something or someone alone, and it is this idea of avoidance that informs the modern meaning of forbear, which is to hold back from something and show patience. Our forebears are our distant ancestors.

I try to forbear making snap decisions until I have all the facts.

My forebears were landed gentry but successive generations squandered all their wealth.

∼

Fordone: The old-fashioned sense of the verb to fordo meant to destroy or do away with something. This verb form has all but disappeared from usage and a secondary meaning in past participle form of fordone means to be overcome with exhaustion.

Many of the runners were fordone by the extreme heat and humidity.

∼

Frap: In Middle English to frap meant to beat or strike somebody; frap them on the nose, for example. The word also means to tighten something with ropes or cables, such as to frap down a tent with guy lines or to frap the sails on a boat.

He thought it best to frap down the marquee in case the wind got up overnight.

∼

Fribble: A rather amusing word that first appeared in English during the nineteenth century. A tendency to fribble means to while away time doing inconsequential things when there are more pressing (but tedious) tasks to be done.

She fribbled away the whole morning browsing the internet.

~

Frisson: Frisson, meaning a brief moment of excitement, a shudder or a thrill, comes from the French word for shiver, *frisson*, deriving from the Latin *frictio* for friction.

She felt a frisson of excitement when opening her gift.

~

Frounce: Derived from the Middle English word *frouncen*, meaning to wrinkle or frown, to frounce something is to crease it deliberately, as with pleats in a dress for example.

The wedding dress was beautifully designed with intricately frounced lace decorations.

~

Frugal: To be frugal is to be sparing or economical with regard to money or food and general expenditure. It is a polite way of describing stinginess and penny-pinching.

His frugal nature didn't allow him to ever send Christmas cards to his family.

~

Frugivorous: Any type of animal, especially mammals that eat fruit as a key component of their diet.

Orang-utans are largely frugivorous but also eat insects and plants.

~

Fubsy: The first known use of the word *fubs*, meaning a chubby person, was in 1780. The word is now obsolete but lives on in the adjective derived from it.

He was rather fubsy before he went on a strict diet.

~

Fulminate: The Latin word for a lightning strike is *fulmantus*. When the word fulminate entered into English in the fifteenth century it was used mainly to describe religious denunciations issued by church authorities – presumably, like lightning strikes, these were seen as acts of God. In modern usage, fulminate means to issue formal denunciations, often politically motivated, or to rail against something or someone with censure and invective.

The Green Party fulminated against current government environmental policy.

～

Fulsome (1) versus Fulsome (2) versus Fulsome (3) versus Fulsome (4): Fulsome (1) initially meant copious or abundant, as in a fulsome crop of vegetables. Over time this connection with foodstuffs led to fulsome (2) gaining the meaning of somebody of large frame on account of their fulsome appetite. At some point, however, this sense of unabashed opulence began to take on a pejorative meaning. Suddenly to be fulsome (3) in praise or reverence was to be over the top and effusive to the point of being sycophantic. Conversely, to be fulsome (4) in welcoming somebody also came to mean being kind, helpful and comforting. So is fulsome positive or negative? It can clearly be used in various ways according to context, so in a sense it is four adjectives in one.

I've had a fulsome (1) crop of winter vegetables in my garden this year.

The fulsome (2) frame of the Hungarian wrestler was a sight to behold.

He was a fulsome (3) fellow, inclined to overt flattery in pursuit of his desires.

We received a fulsome (4) welcome from the hotel staff, who really couldn't do enough for us.

～

Furacious and Furtive: The Latin word for thief is *fur* and it is from this that the word furacious derives, meaning thief-like. The word furtive also derives from thief but in modern English has come to mean any behaviour considered sneaky or underhand.

The furacious actions of tax evaders are tantamount to defrauding the Treasury.

~

Furcate: Something that furcates branches out like a fork (see also Bifurcate).

The Amazon furcates into many smaller tributaries.

~

Fusillade: Borrowed from the French word *fusiller*, meaning to shoot a volley from a musket, a fusillade originally meant rapid fire of shots from a weapon. The word has come to have a figurative sense to describe a barrage of criticism.

The director's latest film was met with a fusillade of criticism.

~

Fuzzle: Derived from the Old German word *fuseln*, meaning to drink alcohol (usually cheap liquor), to fuzzle or be fuzzled is to intoxicate with booze.

A chance meeting in the street led to an impromptu trip to a nearby bar to get fuzzled.

G

~

Gabelle: The gabelle was a tax levied on salt in France, which was finally repealed in 1790. In a general sense a gabelle is any taxation, particularly related to commodities, that is enforced between countries or paid by non-natives.

Airport taxation is a form of gabelle charged to travellers.

~

Gainsay: In Old English, *gēan* meant to go against or opposite to. By the Middle English period *gēan* had become *gain*, and with the addition of 'say' we get gainsay, meaning to speak against or contradict.

The defendant made no attempts to gainsay the prosecution's accusations or evidence, despite pleading not guilty.

∾

Galimatias: A direct borrowing from French, galimatias is unintelligible use of language, especially in speech, e.g. gibberish. The origin of the word is uncertain other than that it is believed to have first been coined by the French Renaissance philosopher Michel de Montaigne in one of his famous essays.

I couldn't understand a word he was saying; it was just galimatias.

∾

Gallimaufry: A *gallimafree* in Middle French was a type of stew made by throwing anything close to hand into the pot. Gallimaufry has since become a literary term for a hotchpotch of different styles or influences all thrown together.

The writer's first few novels were a gallimaufry of different styles and genres.

∾

Galoot: A galoot is an American English slang term for a man or boy who is usually physically large but awkward and possibly of limited intelligence.

Although many people regarded him as something of a galoot, he was kind-hearted and shy.

∾

Garble: When we garble something (usually in speech) we distort it, sometimes wilfully, sometimes unwittingly. However, the origin of the word is from the Arabic word *gharbala*, which was the process of sifting or sieving spices to take out the impurities. It is curious then that when the word came into Middle English as *garbelen* (meaning to separate the best) it should somehow develop a very different meaning in modern English.

I turned on the radio but all I could hear was a mess of garbled sounds.

~

Garrulous: The Latin word *garrulus* means to babble or chatter and translates directly into English as garrulous. There are several adjectives to describe the propensity to talk a lot but garrulous implies somebody in love with the sound of their own voice who often talks tediously or pointlessly.

His garrulous ability to dominate the conversation spoiled the date.

~

Gaucherie: A gaucherie is an awkward, clumsy or tactless social act or comment. Derived from French, it has its root in the word for left, *gauche*. The negative connotation possibly springs from old superstitions about left-handed people being ungainly or accident prone.

Many people seem oblivious to the gaucheries they commit when they express their opinions on social media.

~

Gauleiter: *Gaus* were the name for regional political parties in Nazi Germany. Originally, the word *gauleiter* just meant regional party official (*Leiter* is German for leader). Since the end of the Second World War, however, the word has taken on a euphemistic sense for anybody who is arrogant, overbearing or bullying in nature.

I don't like my new boss at all; she's a real gauleiter!

~

Giglet: Derived from the Middle English word *gigelot*, giglet is a rather unflattering old-fashioned term for a girl of frivolous temperament and often wanton promiscuity.

The pubs and bars of the Whitechapel area were rife with prostitutes and giglets in the late nineteenth century.

~

Gimcrack: A gimcrack is an ornamental object of little use or value. There are several similar words that mean more or less the same thing, such as bauble, knickknack and kickshaw. The word gimcrack first established itself in the English language in the seventeenth century, although the origin of the word is unknown.

My mother is a hoarder of gimcracks; her front room is like a garage sale.

≈

Girn: To girn is a Scottish dialectal word for showing a snarling grin and is thought to be a development of the Middle English *grinnen*.

I'm sure that dog is girning at me.

≈

Glabrous: A surface that is smooth can be described as glabrous. The Latin word *glaber*, meaning bald or without hair, is the root of the word, although in scientific terminology glabrous often refers to parts of the body that have never had any hair, rather than had it and lost it.

The man at the table looked hot and bothered; beads of sweat ran down his glabrous head.

≈

Glissade: To glissade is from the French word *glisser*, meaning to glide. The glissade is an elegant, gliding step in ballet and also a rather dangerous sport involving sliding down a snow-covered mountain without the aid of any skis.

A man was killed glissading down a slope when he lost his ice pick and plunged over a precipice.

≈

Gloaming: A term that derives from the Old English *glōm*, which was the word for twilight or dusk. From Old English the word went north of the border into Scottish dialects, where the gloaming became the moments just before sundown.

Gloaming settings are a standard atmospheric device in Scandinavian crime dramas.

≈

Gnomic: A word which has nothing to do with gnomes, gnomic can mean expressing an idea or concept or truth in a brief, pithy and memorable sentence (see Aphorism) or can also be something which is ambiguous and difficult to fully understand, like most aphorisms.

His gnomic pronouncements seem to have the weight of truth but are also at times baffling.

~

Gourmand and Gourmet: A gourmand is a person who eats excessively. There is often a confusion between gourmand and the French borrowing gourmet. The former eats huge quantities without prejudice, the latter is a refined lover of good food.

Elvis Presley was a gourmand who gorged on peanut butter and jelly sandwiches, huge burgers and deep-fried squirrel.

~

Gravamen: Gravamen derives from the Latin verb *gravare*, meaning to burden, and ultimately from the Latin adjective *gravis*, meaning heavy. Fittingly, gravamen refers to the part of a grievance or complaint that gives it weight or substance and it is used in legal documents and publications.

The gravamens presented by the complainant were scrutinized by the court.

~

Gravid: Another weighty word derived from the Latin *gravis* (see Gravamen). Gravid is often used in the context of women in the later stages of pregnancy – literally, heavy with an unborn child. The word can also be applied to animals and especially fish – a gravid sturgeon is one full of eggs for caviar.

He gave up his seat on the bus to an exhausted-looking gravid woman.

~

Grimalkin: In the opening scene of Shakespeare's play *Macbeth* the first witch utters the line: 'I come, Graymalkin!' According to witchcraft folklore, Satan sent 'familiars' to assist witches. Often these familiars took animal shape to disguise their demon form. The witch, rather quaintly, is responding to the calling of her familiar – a grey cat named Malkin. Shakespeare was responsible for adding many words to the English language and grimalkin is one of the more obscure ones. By the eighteenth century, the spelling had changed, with the word being used to describe any, usually elderly, domestic cat.

> *First Witch*   *Where the place?*
> *Second Witch*   *Upon the heath.*
> *Third Witch*   *There to meet with Macbeth.*
> *First Witch*   *I come, Graymalkin!*
>
> William Shakespeare, *Macbeth*, Act 1, Scene 1

∾

Grubble: To grubble is to grope around in the dark for something. The origin of the word is uncertain but it could be an extension of the Middle English *grubben*, meaning to dig or rummage.

> *I spent half an hour grubbling around in the back of the van trying to find my door keys.*

∾

Guerdon: The first known recording of guerdon is in Chaucer's *The Romaunt of the Rose* (*circa* 1366): 'He quitte him wel his guerdon there.' A guerdon is a reward or a recompense for something and can be used as both a noun and a verb (give or receive a guerdon). The origins of the term are the Old German word for reward, *widarlōn*. Shakespeare also uses the word in *Love's Labour's Lost* in a scene in which the clown Costard is given money for delivering love letters but fails to realize that guerdon and remuneration are synonymous.

> *'Guerdon, O sweet guerdon! Better than remuneration; eleven-pence farthing better: most sweet guerdon!'*
>
> William Shakespeare, *Love's Labour's Lost*, Act 3, Scene 1

∾

Gulosity: The Latin adjective *gulosus*, meaning gluttonous, is the source of gulosity, a rare synonym for gluttony and excessive appetite. Samuel Johnson is often erroneously cited as the first person to coin the word, as it appears in his famous dictionary. Given its Latin roots the word almost certainly existed in English long before Johnson's time, and the connection is probably more a reflection of the doctor's lavish eating habits.

I was disgusted by the gulosity of my nephews; they shovel down food like it is their last meal on earth.

Gumption: Although the exact origin of the word is unknown, gumption has been used in the English language since the early 1700s to mean intelligence or common sense. In the 1860s American English speakers also used it to refer to tenacity.

Although she had never attempted to assemble flat-pack furniture before, with a bit of time and gumption she successfully managed it.

H

Habiliments: Habiliments are items of clothing particular to an occasion or a particular profession, such as formal evening wear or a military uniform. The word derives from the Old French word *abiller*, meaning to prepare.

The Queen was adorned in her usual regal habiliments for the State Opening of Parliament.

Haematic: The old Greek word for blood, *haima*, is the root for many words relating to medicine. Haematic is no exception and describes anything resembling, containing or generally relating to blood.

The wine had a deep, dark, almost haematic colouring.

Halcyon: In Greek mythology, Alkyone, the daughter of Aeolus, the god of the winds, became so distraught when she learned that her husband had been killed in a shipwreck that she threw herself into the sea and was changed into a kingfisher. The Ancient Greeks named kingfishers *alkyon* or *halcyon*. Legend has it that when kingfishers nest in winter they help to calm the rough seas and so halcyon has come to mean a period of calm and relief from worry and stress.

She often recalled the halcyon days of her childhood.

Hallowed: Hallowed means holy or consecrated and was being used in the English language prior to the twelfth century. Descending from the Old English *hālig*, meaning holy, and later Middle English *halowen*, All Hallows' Day was the name for what Christians now call All Saints' Day (the day before this being Halloween).

His body was buried in hallowed ground.

Haply: In the Middle Ages anything that happened by chance, random good luck or accident was described as haply. The root is from the Old Norse word *happ*, meaning luck or good fortune. In modern speech the word has become interchangeable with happily, though in fact there is a subtle difference in meaning and usage. For example, *I lost my wallet but* haply *someone found it and handed it in* (it was lucky someone found it and was honest). *I lost my wallet but* happily *someone found it and handed it in* (the person finding the wallet was happy – found it in a happy manner).

Harbinger: A noun with multiple meanings through history, several of which have become lost over time. Originally, in the twelfth century, travellers would send a harbinger ahead to procure board and lodgings for the night. This meaning gradually evolved into the use of harbinger as a host (the meaning of the French word *harbierge*) and also relates to the meaning of the verb to harbour. The modern meaning of harbinger is something or someone that foreshadows or predicts future events or actions, as in the phrase 'a harbinger of doom'.

The recent nice weather should not be taken as a harbinger of brighter days to come.

≈

Hardihood: Hardihood is strength, vigour and resolve and is related to the shorter adjective hardy, meaning resolute and stalwart.

The famous explorers had the hardihood to persevere in the face of often intolerable conditions.

≈

Hariolation: A scholarly word derived from the Latin verb *hariolatio* – the action of prophesying. Hariolations are deductions based upon guesswork not necessarily supported by facts or evidence.

The latest theories on the decline of the dinosaurs were dismissed as mere hariolations.

≈

Hauteur: Hauteur comes from the French word *haut*, meaning high or top. Other French words common in English from the same family are *haute couture* (high fashion) and *haute cuisine* (high food/dining). People exhibiting hauteur certainly have a high opinion of themselves, usually exhibiting arrogance and pomposity in their manner.

The hauteur exhibited by the duke's new wife was not in keeping with her modest upbringing.

≈

Hebdomadal: A complex-sounding word with a rather humdrum meaning. It relates to the calendar week and derives from *hepta*, the Greek word for seven. Something hebdomadal occurs weekly.

On Fridays she made her hebdomadal trip to the supermarket.

≈

Hebetate and Hebetude: The Latin word *hebes* means dull and so to hebetate something is to make it dull, uninspiring and/or crush the spirit out of it. Hebetude is naturally the noun for the end result of this process and is often related to lethargy and listless apathy of the mind.

Young people spending too much time on electronic devices leads to hebetude and indolence.

~

Helminthophobia and Helminthagogue: *Helminth* is the Greek word for worms and, as with all phobias, the Greek word for fear is the suffix. This particular phobia relates to the morbid fear of having the body infested with parasitic worms. Should such an unfortunate and unpleasant occurrence happen, a medical professional can administer a helminthagogue (medical stimulant) to dispel the nasty critters from the intestinal tracts.

Helminthophobia is an irrational fear of contracting a tapeworm.

~

Hemiplegia: A large number of medical terms in English derive from Greek. *Hemi* means half and *plegia* paralysis, thus hemiplegia is paralysis of one side of the body, often as a consequence of a brain injury.

The motorcycle accident left him with hemiplegia on his left side.

~

Hendecasyllabic: Hendecasyllabic describes a poem or more commonly a line of poetry that adheres to a strict metre of eleven syllables. *Hendeka* is the Greek word for the number eleven.

Victorian poets such as Tennyson and Swinburne experimented with hendecasyllabic verse.

~

Hepcat: This is a hipster with knowledge of the latest fashions and music who always keeps up with the latest lingo on the streets.

I'm not cool enough to go to those clubs; they are only for the hepcats.

❦

Hesperidate: In Ancient Greek mythology, Hesperides was a beautiful garden guarded by nymphs that contained trees bearing golden fruit. It was said to lie in the westernmost part of the world and produced the fruit given as a wedding present by Gaia to Hera on the occasion of her marriage to Zeus. The adjective hesperidate can be used as a classical allusion to any garden or orchard with beautiful fruit trees.

In autumn the gardens fill with a hesperidate glow of golden colours.

❦

Hinny: A synonym for a mule, a cross between a donkey and a horse. Curiously, in Scottish dialect calling someone a hinny is a term of endearment usually reserved for children and young women.

My hinny isn't well, hinny. We are going to have to fetch a vet.

❦

Hirsute: Hirsutism is a medical condition where hair grows in uncommon places on the human body. This has led to the slightly derogatory term hirsute being used to describe somebody who has excessive bodily hair.

When he got out of the swimming pool I noticed how hirsute he was.

❦

Homograph, Homonym and Homophone: All three words relate to the spelling and sounds of words that are similar but mean different things. Homographs are words spelt the same and pronounced the same but with different meanings. Homonyms are words spelt the same but pronounced differently to produce different meanings. Homophones are words with a different spelling but the same pronunciation.

I hate quail eggs; they make me quail. (Homograph)

She wound the bandage round the wound. (Homonym)

Show our two guests to their room but don't take too long. (Homophone)

∼

Homologate: To homologate is to agree to, confirm or allow something via official sanction. A registrar, for example, homologates a marriage and judges do all sorts of homologating in the law courts. *Homos* in Greek means same or alike and *logos* means word, so in essence a homologate is agreeing with the same words.

The judge refused to homologate the defendant's plea bargain.

∼

Hooey: A word of North American origin, possibly of southern dialect meaning nonsense or rubbish, and used as a polite alternative to saying 'crap' or 'shit'.

I wouldn't bother watching that film; it's a load of hooey.

∼

Hope versus Hopefully: 'Hope springs eternal' Alexander Pope wrote hopefully in his work *An Essay on Man* (1733). What exactly does this sentence mean? The problem lies with the definition and misuse of a word that divides opinion among language gurus and pedants: 'hopefully'. The traditional meaning of hopefully is 'to hope for' something to occur. It is thought that the word came into English from German settlers in the eighteenth and nineteenth centuries. The German word that most closely resembles hopefully is *hoffentlich*, which is used in the German language as a floating sentence modifier to express phrases such as 'with any luck'. It is easy to see how, over time, *hoffentlich* mutated into the English word hopefully and came to be used in a similar way, as in 'hopefully it won't rain tomorrow'. The main objection to this usage is that hopefully isn't functioning as an adverb in the example above because it isn't modifying the verb in the sentence. Grammar purists have suggested that alternatives such as 'It is to be hoped it won't rain' are technically correct. The correct use of hopefully should be to do something in a hopeful manner: 'She gazed hopefully into the distance.' In formal writing it is considered to be stylistically sloppy but it is so prevalent in everyday speech that it's almost impossible to escape it.

While Pope, in his famous phrase, was expressing the virtue of retaining hope against adversity and the belief that it is to be hoped that things will get better, he was also writing hopefully.

∾

Horary: An old-fashioned alternative to describe something occurring hourly, derived from the Latin *hora*, meaning hour.

He was kept awake all night by the horary chimes of the church clock.

∾

Horripilation and Horripilate: Essentially a literary word much used by gothic novelists of the nineteenth century, horripilation is the sensation of the hairs on the skin bristling due to cold, fear or excitement. Derived from the Latin *horrēre*, meaning to stand on end, plus *pilus*, hair, horripilation can also be used to describe goose bumps.

Walking through the graveyard caused the hairs on his neck to horripilate.

∾

Hortative: Hortative can be used as both an adjective and a noun, although the latter form has become increasingly rare. When we provide a hortative sentence we are urging or advising somebody about a future course of action or situation.

He was happy to provide a hortative to anyone asking his advice.

∾

Hoyden and Hoydenish: In Middle Dutch (around the fifteenth century) a *heyden* was a boisterous and uncouth young man. The term hoyden is an old-fashioned word for a tomboy or rather loud young woman. Etymologists speculate that hoyden possibly developed as a feminine form of *heyden*. The adjective hoydenish describes the behaviour of a hoyden.

My daughter has always been something of a hoyden and has refused to wear a skirt or a dress since she was four years old.

~

Hubris: Derived from the Greek word *hybris*, meaning excessive pride and self-confidence, often ill-placed, the meaning of hubris is identical in English. In Ancient Greek tragedy, hubris was seen as a character flaw that was the undoing of many tragic heroes such as Achilles and Oedipus.

The hubris exhibited by Hitler in the final years of the war was ultimately the Nazis' undoing.

~

Hyaline: In Greek *hyalinus* refers to glass-like substances. In English the adjective hyaline describes objects or substances that are transparent or glass-like.

The sun shone through the hyaline sheets of Perspex set into the walls.

~

Hyetography: Hyetography is the study, usually over distinct periods of time, of the distribution and frequency of rainfall.

It always impresses people at parties when she tells them she studied hyetography for her PhD.

~

Hymeneal: The hymeneal was originally the song or songs sung at wedding ceremonies – think of it as the song played for the bride and groom's 'first dance' at modern wedding receptions. As an adjective it can relate to any aspect of a wedding. Hymen was the Greek god of marriage.

We decided to keep the hymeneal vows at our wedding service short and sweet given that we had both been married before.

~

Hyperaesthesia: A truly debilitating condition, hyperaesthesia is an abnormal or pathological increase in stimulation of the senses, such as of the skin to touch, the ear to loud sound frequencies or the eyes to bright lights.

Many military personnel suffering from post-traumatic stress disorder develop hyperaesthesia.

∾

Hyperbole: Originally, hyperbole was a technical term in the study of rhetoric, but over time it has come into modern usage. A commonly mispronounced word, hyperbole derived from the Greek word *hyperbolē*, meaning to exceed. The addition of the macron (a small slash above the e) denotes that the word should be pronounced with a long vowel sound. Hyperbole is deliberate and often extravagant use of exaggeration in speech or written language, frequently used for persuasive effect.

It drives me crazy when people mispronounce the word hyperbole.

∾

Hyperborean: In ancient mythology the Hyperboreans were a race of people who lived in the far north of the world in a land of perpetual daylight. In Greek, *boreas* was the north wind and *hyper* means above and beyond. In modern English, hyperborean (in lower case) functions as an adjective to describe areas of the earth, northern countries such as Greenland and the polar caps, that experience constant daylight for periods of the year.

During the hyperborean months of summer, insomnia can become a problem for travellers unaccustomed to constant daylight.

∾

Hypogeal: Hypogeal relates to things that grow or live below the surface and is an alternative synonym to subterranean. The two words are more or less interchangeable except that hypogeal relates to living things whereas subterranean merely means beneath the ground.

Hypogeal plants germinate below the surface of the earth.

∾

Hysteresis: Hysteresis is a term in physics that means a lack of response by a body to changes in forces acting upon it, particularly magnetic fields. The word derives from *hysteresis* in Greek, which means to be lagging behind.

Owing to hysteresis the part of the band magnetized is not symmetrically placed with regard to the magnetic poles.

I

Iambic: Iambic is a poetic term referring to the pattern of words in lines of verse. An iamb is a metrical foot consisting of one short syllable followed by one long syllable, or of one unstressed syllable followed by one stressed syllable. Shakespeare popularized the iambic pentameter form consisting of lines of five sets of unstressed syllables followed by stressed syllables.

'But, soft! what light through yonder window breaks?'
William Shakespeare, *Romeo and Juliet*, Act 2, Scene 2

Ichor: The Ancient Greeks used the word *ichōr* to describe an unearthly liquid that runs through the veins of the gods in place of human blood. In medical terms, ichor denotes thin watery discharges that contain traces of blood.

Ichor is often a symptom of stomach ulcers.

Iconoclast and Iconoclastic: An iconoclast was traditionally defined as a person who destroys religious images or opposes their veneration. The word derives from the Greek *eikonoklastēs*, which literally translates as image destructor.

The critic was renowned for his controversial, iconoclastic views.

Ictus: The Latin word *icere*, meaning to strike or blow, provides the root for this word, which denotes repetitive beats or sound patterns.

The complex ictus in the arrangements seemed more improvised than designed.

~

Ideologue: A relatively young word in English, which entered from the French word *ideologue*, meaning an ideologist. In English, however, the word ideologue often refers to somebody who has blind adherence to a particular point of view.

The euphoria following the revolution proved to be a false dawn as impractical ideologues took control.

~

Idoneous: An idoneous person is somebody who fits the bill: they are suitable and proper, the best person for the job or situation.

Finally, after years of dating, she found the idoneous partner.

~

Igneous: The Latin word for fire, *ignis*, provides the root for the adjective igneous, which relates to anything fiery. In geology igneous is often used in relation to volcanic activity and the movement of magma – hence igneous rock formations.

The areas are hot spots for earthquakes and fiery igneous volcanoes.

~

Illapse: A sophisticated word meaning the gliding or sliding of one thing into another or to fall or flow.

The illapse of new words into the English language shows no sign of abating.

~

Immanent: Something which is immanent is inherent and in a sense all-pervading in a subject or being.

The immanent beauty of nature is beyond question.

~

Immure: The Latin word for a wall is *murus* and this provides the root for mural, a wall painting. To immure is to entomb or place something in a wall. Immure also has a general sense of somebody being walled in somewhere in a figurative sense.

Ever since he bought that games console my son has been immured in his bedroom for hours on end.

~

Immutable: Immutable derives from the Latin *immutabilis*, meaning unable to change. The modern sense of immutable is something that is set in stone, so to speak, and cannot be altered or changed.

There are immutable guidelines for dealing with such situations.

~

Impecunious: The state of being impecunious is a sorry one indeed, as it involves having little or no money. One curious aspect of the word is that its antonym, pecunious, is very rarely used in English and has disappeared from some dictionaries. This may possibly be due to some confusion over the word's meaning. It would be natural to assume that a pecunious person was wealthy but on the few occasions the word appears in print it is usually in the context of miserliness.

I was impecunious throughout my student years and don't know how I survived.

~

Impel: Although often synonymous with the verb to compel, impel suggests to drive forward to action by, or according to, strong moral pressures and concerns. The word is also related to impulse, although impel suggests considered decision making.

He felt impelled to speak up against the injustices he felt were prevalent in society.

~

Impercipient: The adjective impercipient can be applied to anyone who seems to lack any ability to perceive. It is often used in relation to an inability to understand a given concept or idea, as opposed to the traditional definition of lack of perception as being an inability to comprehend through the senses.

His explanation of spirituality shows an impercipient view of the wider contexts.

~

Imperium: *Imperium* is a Latin word that translates as the power to command, or the absolute power to rule over a dominion. In Ancient Rome, *imperium* related to the right to command the military.

It is a characteristic of tyrants to exert their imperium early in the reign.

~

Imperturbable: The Latin word *perturbare* means to confuse. Peculiarly, the word imperturbable, a person exuding calm and measured behaviour and character, predates its opposite (perturbed) by several hundred years. Possibly the onset of industrialization caused people to become more confused and stressed.

Despite the many problems and issues he had encountered, he displayed an imperturbable attitude towards his affairs.

~

Impetrate: To impetrate originally meant to entreat or beg, often via prayer, for something to pass or happen. The word derives from the Latin *patrare*, meaning to accomplish.

It seems hypocritical to impetrate God for help and guidance if you don't really believe in religion.

~

Imply versus Infer: If a speaker or writer implies something, they are suggesting it in an indirect way rather than making an explicit statement. The reader or listener is then left to draw their own conclusions from what has been said or hinted at, thereby inferring the meaning. The two words are often used interchangeably but this can become confusing. If, for example, somebody took exception to an inference in something they read or heard, they would be correct to question what was being implied, but incorrect to challenge the inference.

He implied that the general had been a traitor.

I inferred from his words that the general had been a traitor.

❧

Impolitic: The antonym of impolitic is, naturally, politic, which comes from the French/Latin term *politicus*, meaning shrewd and tactful. Impolitic has logically come to mean untactful and ill-judged actions and words; in the realm of politics, policies by administrations that are adverse to the common good.

He was indiscreet in utterance, impolitic in management, opinionated, self-confident and uncompromising in nature and methods.

❧

Imprest: An imprest is an archaic term for a loan or money advance. The origin is uncertain but it could possibly be from the Italian word *imprestare*, meaning to lend.

I may have to beseech my boss for an imprest before pay day.

❧

Impudicity: To have impudicity is to have a sense of shamelessness, often in contrast to received wisdom or taste or common decency.

The impudicity of the rotund middle-aged man cavorting in his swimming shorts offended several of the hotel guests.

❧

Impugn: The Latin verb *pugnare* means to fight. It is also the root for words such as pugnacious, meaning aggressive and confrontational. To impugn somebody is to verbally assail them with a barrage of criticisms or rebuttals.

I impugned him over his behaviour, which was unacceptable.

~

Incandescent: A relatively young word, incandescent first appeared in the English language in the eighteenth century. Developing technology entailed various experiments in science involving how best to harness sources of sustaining heat and light. Anything that glowed in the course of this experimentation was declared incandescent. The word has its root in the Latin verb *candēre*, meaning to shine or glow (candle has the same stem). However, once the word had established itself, over the next two hundred years everything that glowed or shone, both literally and figuratively, could be described as incandescent: incandescent wit, incandescent stage performances, people being incandescent with rage etc.

I was mesmerized by the incandescent colours of the northern lights.

~

Inchoate: In Latin *inchoare* means to start work on something or describes something to be worked on. In English inchoate is used to describe something incoherent or only partially formed, such as a plan or idea, and has a sense that starting work on it (in the Latin sense) wouldn't make much difference.

The computer programmer had a hard time locating the system error because its appearance was random and inchoate.

~

Inconcinnity and Incongruity: Inconcinnity and incongruity are close in meaning but differ slightly in how they should be applied. Both words derive from their antonyms, concinnity and congruity, which have their roots in Latin. *Concinnitās* means skilfully and harmoniously constructed and relates principally to written discourse. *Congruus* means in agreement, in harmony and correspondence. Inconcinnity is therefore a muddled discourse where the elements lack harmony or a logical structure. Incongruity also means disharmony but can be applied to any composition of features where one or more aspects disagrees with and disrupts the whole.

The placing of a mock-Tudor house in the middle of the new estate displayed blatant incongruity.

~

Incondite: Often used in relation to language this word can be applied to any object, such as buildings or flat-pack furniture; incondite means badly constructed or put together.

It is depressing but there is something about an incondite argument or sentence which really makes me weep.

~

Indeciduous: The opposite of deciduous and, like its antonym, it can also be used figuratively (see Deciduous). Indeciduous is often mistakenly used as a synonym for indecisive.

The planting of indeciduous trees ensured that the gardens didn't appear too barren in winter.

~

Indign: Indign describes somebody who is unworthy or undeserving of something. The word has an archaic related meaning, now largely obsolete, of somebody behaving in a manner unbecoming to their status.

After such a lacklustre performance the disputed late goal only served to underline that the home team were indign winners of the tournament.

~

Indocile: A docile person is quiet and compliant and does what they are told to do. An indocile person is difficult to instruct or influence and often a disruptive influence.

My French class was full of indocile pupils.

~

Indwell: Indwell is an archaic verb that hails from the fourteenth century when there were common beliefs around spirits, both good and evil, that acted as forces upon human life by indwelling the soul. The word is thought to have been first coined by the theologian John Wycliffe (1320–84) in his ground-breaking Bible translations and philosophical writings. Ironically, following his death, Wycliffe was renounced as a heretic for being spiritually bereft and his corpse was exhumed from consecrated ground and burned.

Open your soul and let the power and love of God indwell.

~

Ineffable versus Unspeakable: How to describe a word that means 'cannot be described in words'? Ineffable comes from the Latin *ineffabilis*, meaning incapable of being expressed. The word is sometimes used to describe taboos or things that should not be spoken of: ineffable subjects. Similarly, it is also used as a synonym for unspeakable. However, ineffable is a positive adjective, such as when we refer to the ineffable beauty of a natural phenomenon. Unspeakable is much harsher and negative, applied, for example, in relation to the unspeakable horrors of war.

Many travel writers have struggled with the ineffable beauty of America's National Parks.

~

Inexpugnable: In Latin *inexpugnabilis* was a term often used to describe military fortifications that were difficult or impossible to 'take by storm'. In English, the word inexpugnable is often used to describe leaders, usually dictators and despots, whose grip on power is so strong they cannot be overthrown. A secondary, more positive use, is in relation to fixed and stable ideas that will never change.

He had an inexpugnable belief in the essential goodness of people.

~

Ingeminate: A rare verb that has been superseded by its synonym reiterate. Derived from the Latin *ingemināre*, meaning to repeat, ingeminate means to restate in words.

Several times during the debate, the treasurer ingeminated the government's position on the economy.

~

Ingénue: An ingénue is a naïve young woman, seemingly innocent in the ways of the world. The word is believed to have first been coined in English by William Makepeace Thackeray in *Vanity Fair* (1848) in describing the novel's scheming anti-hero Becky Sharp. Ingénue is often applied to a particular character in melodramas depicting a young but ambitious actress yearning for wealth and status.

> *'When attacked sometimes, Becky had a knack of adopting a demure* ingénue *air, under which she was most dangerous.'*
>
> William Makepeace Thackeray, *Vanity Fair* (1848)

~

Inimical versus Inimitable: A common error is to confuse these two words, as they sound very alike, but they mean radically different things. Inimical derives from the Latin word for enemy – *inimicus*. Inimical forces are malevolent and hostile and wish to do harm. Inimitable, on the other hand, means something that can't be copied or imitated, like the inimitable guitar playing of Jimi Hendrix.

> *She flashed him a hard, inimical stare.*

> *It was a stellar performance delivered in the group's own inimitable style.*

~

Inordinate: Derived from the Latin verb *ordinare*, meaning to arrange or organize, the original meaning of inordinate was to describe something unregulated or disorderly. This meaning has been replaced by a wider sense of something being excessive or unusually large in size or duration.

> *An inordinate amount of time was wasted achieving the most menial of tasks.*

~

Inquietude: To suffer from inquietude is to be in a state of mental disturbance and restlessness, like noises in the brain, and a lack of calmness and psychological agitation.

> *Following the death of his father he slipped into a period of anxious inquietude.*

≈

Inquiline: Derived from the Latin word *inquilīnus*, meaning lodger or tenant, this is a zoological term that refers to a creature that lives in the abode of another. Inquilines differ from parasites in that their presence is not usually harmful or negative to the host animal. The word inquiline could feasibly be used to describe somebody living in another person's house.

Birds' nests can act as habitats for inquiline species, which may not affect the bird directly.

≈

Insensate: The Latin word *sensatus* means to have senses. Lack of sense can also be a lack of sensitivity and hence insensate has different contexts. A person can be insensate because they lack common sense or because they lack sensitivity or empathy.

My insensate boss insisted I work late on my child's birthday.

≈

Insentient: Insentient relates to the senses, perception and consciousness. An insentient person is incapable of feeling or comprehending things. In a wider sense, insentient is sometimes used to describe people who lack sensitivity.

It is a presumption that animals are insentient and lack consciousness.

≈

Insouciant: A word of French origin formed with the negative prefix *in* and *souciant*, meaning to be troubled or concerned, so literally 'not bothered'. Modern usage of the word often implies affectation by somebody towards a particular situation or event, possibly to save face.

He adopted an insouciant attitude when he lost his job at the abattoir.

≈

Intercession: An intercession is the act of interceding on behalf of someone. A secondary meaning of intercession is a petition or prayer in support of something or someone; the Pope, for example, may make an intercession in support of the victims of an earthquake.

She faced ruin but the intercession of her friends made the authorities reconsider.

~

Interlard: The original meaning of interlard came from France, where it was a culinary term for mixing alternate layers of meat with fat. Although rarely used, in modern English to interlard something (usually a speech or piece of writing) is to embellish it with different elements to make it more diverse and striking, or, in keeping with the word's original meaning, add flavour and texture.

The professor liked to interlard his lectures with personal anecdotes.

~

Interlocutor: Interlocutor derives from the Latin *loqui*, meaning to speak, with the prefix *inter*, meaning between (speak between). An interlocutor is somebody engaged in a dialogue or conversation.

Russia acts as a frequent interlocutor between its allies in Syria and Iran and the other Arab states.

~

Intorsion: Intorsion is a medical term for the rotation of a body part around an axis or a fixed point. It can also refer explicitly to the eyes, so rolling or crossing one's eyes is a form of intorsion.

The physiotherapist taught her some intorsion exercises to help with the trapped nerves in her shoulder.

~

Intromit: To intromit is to allow, permit, send or cause entry or access into somewhere. Lavish balls thrown by the aristocracy would employ an intromitter to call out the names of the invited guests as they entered the party. On a more mundane level, placing a coin in a slot to raise a traffic barrier is an act of intromitting.

She's always wanted to go to a really posh party where they intromit you before you enter.

≈

Inveigle: Another untrustworthy word, literally speaking. To inveigle has two meanings in current usage: either to gain entrance to somewhere or to persuade somebody to do something as a joint enterprise or as an initially unwilling accomplice. The key is that both usages are dripping with deception and falsehood. Derived from a hybrid of Old French and early modern English, an *enveegler* was a swindler or confidence trickster who used charming patter and flattery for their own ends.

They inveigled their way into the nightclub with false ID cards.

With the promise of future riches, he tried to inveigle them to invest in the pyramid investment scheme.

≈

Inviolate and Inviolable: When we make a solemn promise to keep a secret, it should be inviolate – that is, cannot be corrupted or broken. Inviolate can also mean something free from violation, pure and undisturbed. A less common alternative is inviolable, which has the same meaning.

When I was six years old I made an inviolate pledge to my best friend to stay friends forever.

≈

Irruption versus Eruption: The noun form of the intransitive verb to irrupt has become neglected in general usage. The word is most commonly used in scientific fields such as botany and zoology to describe a sudden proliferation of a particular species of plant or animal. A possible reason for its scarcity outside of scientific journals is that it is commonly confused and replaced with the word eruption. The difference, although subtle, is none-theless distinct and lies in the prefix. Irruption means to break in or, in a descriptive sense, invade or colonize an area or space, whereas eruption means to break out, as it is prefixed with the Latin-based *ex*.

The vegetable patch suffered from an irruption *of slugs and snails.*

The volcanic eruption *spewed clouds of ash into the atmosphere.*

J

~

Jactation: A word meaning boastful declarations or displays. Jactation is also the word for tossing and turning restlessly when trying to sleep.

As an insomniac, my wife finds my nightly jactations alarming.

~

Janiform: The Ancient Roman god Janus was the god of beginnings and transitions (as well as of gates and doorways). Effigies and statues of Janus usually portray the god as having two faces, one on either side of his head to signify looking into the future and the past simultaneously. The adjective janiform means something with two faces, such as a double-headed coin.

The house was adorned with plaster effigies of ancient gods, including a janiform bust over the doorway.

~

Jark: A jark was a medieval word for a fake seal or stamp on an official document.

The experts determined the ancient documents were forgeries by examining the jarks.

~

Jaunce: To jaunce is an archaic equestrian word and describes the skill of persuading a horse to prance. The jaunce is a recognized movement in the sport of dressage.

When the colt saw the young filly in the field, he suddenly seemed to jaunce around with his head carried high.

~

Jectigation: Jectigation came into English from French via Latin and means a wagging gesture of the fingers or tremulous shaking of the hands.

The headmaster gave jectigations with his fingers to emphasize the key points of his speech.

~

Jeremiad: A jeremiad is a prolonged complaint or bugbear and/or a lamentation about suffering. The word is thought to derive from the Old Testament's Book of Jeremiah. The Hebrew prophet is known for his austere and sombre admonitions against his own people for their false values and bad faith. In the eighteenth century, Jeremiah became a slang term for a naysayer of pious character and it is from this that the noun jeremiad developed as a noun for a long-standing grievance or objection.

There is a jeremiad against elite universities for doing little to provide places for students from under-privileged backgrounds.

~

Jiggery-pokery: Probably deriving from the Scots *jouk* (to dodge or cheat) and *pawk* (trick or wile), jiggery-pokery means underhanded manipulation or dealings and was first used in English around 1900.

No one trusted him as he was renowned for using a degree of jiggery-pokery in his business deals.

~

Jobation: A jobation is a lengthy, tedious and repetitive reprimand. The word first came into English in the seventeenth century and is of uncertain origin, although, similarly to jeremiad, it may relate to the Old Testament. The titular character in the Book of Job faces many tests and hardships and his name in Hebrew means 'persecuted one'. The inference therefore is that a jobation is perhaps an unjustified and unrelenting criticism.

The boss spent the weekly Monday team meeting going through various jobations with his staff.

∾

Jocose: From the Latin *jocosus*, meaning a tendency to joke, jocose is roughly synonymous with other words such as humorous and witty. The subtle distinction is that jocose is usually considered to be a character trait, a tendency not to take things too seriously, whereas witty relates to a quickness of mind.

The jocose character of my uncle always made his visits great fun.

∾

Jongleur: In medieval France and Norman England, a jongleur was an itinerant minstrel who would provide entertainment in the form of songs, humorous stories and acrobatic tricks. The Old French word, *jougleur*, translates as pleasant and smiling, and is also the root word for juggler.

She could sing, she could dance, she could even juggle – a true jongleur in every sense.

∾

Juggins: A pejorative term for somebody simple-minded or idiotic, the origin of juggins has baffled etymologists. The word entered into English in the nineteenth century and it has been speculated that juggins was perhaps the surname of a notorious family (possibly fictional), the Juggins, renowned for their stupidity.

Oh I'm such a juggins, I can't believe I've lost my glasses again.

∾

Jugulate: A rather nasty term, of medical origin (usually used in autopsy reports), to jugulate is to slit somebody's throat.

Colombian drug gangs' favourite form of retribution is to jugulate their victims, hang them upside down and watch them bleed to death.

∾

Juvenescent: A word that first entered into English in the 1800s, largely as a result of a craze for cosmetics, tinctures and miracle cures to prolong a youthful-looking face, juvenescent means to appear to be defying old age and thereby remaining forever young.

Despite his advancing years, the actor has remained popular with young people on account of his juvenescent good looks.

∾

Juxtaposition: The act or an instance of placing two or more elements or aspects side by side, often to compare or contrast them or to create an interesting effect.

I wasn't sure the juxtaposition of roasted meat with stewed fruit really worked for the judges of the culinary competition.

K

Kakorrhaphiophobia: Kakorrhaphiophobia is an abnormal, persistent, irrational fear of failure. In clinical cases, it's debilitating: the fear of even the most subtle failure or defeat is so intense that it restricts a person from doing anything at all.

My neighbour hasn't worked for years due to kakorrhaphiophobia.

∾

Kalon: Kalon is the ideal of physical and moral beauty, especially as conceived by the philosophers of classical Greece, and derives from the Greek word *kalos*, meaning virtuous and beautiful.

His last partner was so lovely but he never seemed to appreciate what a kalon she was until after they split up.

~

Karezza: A modern word from the Italian slang, *karezza*, this means to caress. As its name implies, it's comprised of intimate activities such as gentle stroking, cuddling and skin-to-skin contact.

She saw karezza as a way to promote health and happiness in marriage.

~

Keck: An archaic word for retching which derives from Old English and was first recorded in the thirteenth century. In Chaucer's *The Canterbury Tales*, the Wife of Bath describes the smell of her husband's feet as making her *kecke*.

The smell of raw fish always makes me keck.

~

Kinaesthetic: Kinaesthetic relates to learning through feeling such as a sense of body position, muscle movement and weight as felt through nerve endings. Kinaesthetic can also relate to an individual's learning styles. Some people learn better by doing, as in trial and error, than by aural instruction.

Some students find certain things easier to learn by adopting a kinaesthetic approach.

~

Kitsch: Kitsch was borrowed from German in the 1920s and means something that is tacky or lowbrow, and sometimes of poor quality.

Her plastic Christmas tree earrings were really kitsch, but she loved them!

L

~

Labile: The original meaning of labile was derived from the French word *labile*, meaning prone to make mistakes or slips of judgement. The modern definition is something susceptible to sudden changes (in scientific terms, such as labile substances) or susceptible to change (like the weather in certain climates).

The young age of the region's hills result in labile rock formations, which are susceptible to slippages.

~

Labret: Any facial decoration worn through a perforation in the lips, such as a ring, stud or spike.

Among the Suri and Mursi tribes of Ethiopia it is traditional for young women to have a labret in the form of a clay ring inserted prior to their wedding ceremony.

~

Labyrinthine: Labyrinthine was first used in the English language in the early seventeenth century and describes something labyrinth-like, i.e. intricate or complicated.

A labyrinthine set of clues needed to be solved before completing the puzzle.

~

Lacertilian: Anything that looks like, behaves like or is related in some sense to lizards can be described as lacertilian.

In Fear and Loathing in Las Vegas *there is a memorable scene in which Hunter S. Thompson hallucinates about people with lacertilian heads swarming around the Circus-Circus hotel.*

~

Laches: Predominantly a legal term, laches refers to a failure to comply or observe a right or privilege. The word can also be generally applied to any notable dereliction of duty. It is derived from the Latin *laxare*, meaning to loosen.

The compensation claims against financial companies may get bound up in questions of laches.

~

Lachrymose: Lachrymose is applied to a person given to tears or weeping or something that engenders a sorrowful or mournful response.

The 1970s gave birth to a fashion for lachrymose films, such as Love Story, *which are now regarded as the perfect 'date film'.*

~

Laconic: Laconia was a region of Ancient Greece, home to the fearless Spartans. For several centuries laconic referred to anything related to the Spartan clan. The Spartans were proud and didn't mince their words so became known as being rather abrupt and to the point. The modern meaning of laconic derives from this reputation and relates to terse and concise use of words.

Hemingway's characters are wilfully laconic, their dialogue sparse and pointed.

~

Lacteous, Lactescent, Lactiferous and Lactifluous: From the Latin word for milk, *lact*, comes a whole host of milk-based adjectives. Lacteous is the colour of milk; lactescent the quality of milk (milkiness of the light at sunset etc.); lactiferous the word for something milk bearing; and lactifluous the gush or flow of milk as from a cow's udders.

Gently blend the spices with a little cornflour and water, stirring constantly on a low heat until the sauce has a lactescent consistency.

~

Lacustrine: From the Latin word for lake, *lacus*, lacustrine is anything relating to, formed in, living in or growing in lakes.

Many tourists flock to the Italian lakes to marvel at the stunning lacustrine countryside.

∼

Lagan: *Laganum* was the Latin word for anything washed up by the sea from a shipwreck. During the height of seafaring, cargo ships that ran into difficulties would attach valuable cargo to buoys and toss it into the sea in the hope that it could be recovered or be washed up ashore.

The sailors were able to recover some of the lagan they had lost when the ship went down.

∼

Lagniappe: An unusual word that American writer and man of letters Mark Twain was most taken with. In his *Life on the Mississippi* (1883) Twain describes discovering the word in New Orleans in the French Quarter, where it was customary for traders to give a small gift or a lagniappe to generous customers.

The proprietor at the tobacconist's gave me two lighters as a lagniappe when I bought four cartons of cigarettes.

∼

Laicism: Laicism is a political ideology or programme that either reduces or outlaws religious influence in a country or culture.

Stalin adopted a robust regime of laicism, effectively banning all religious practice.

∼

Lallation: Lallation is similar to lambdacism in that it refers to a speech impediment or tic, but it most commonly describes infants' inability to form words correctly in speech, or problems that elderly people find in doing so when suffering from dementia.

The doctor mentioned the probability of lallation developing as a consequence of my aunt's stroke.

∾

Lambdacism: Lambdacism is a speech impediment or verbal tic where the sound 'l' is confused with or substituted for other phonemes.

I thought he just couldn't remember my name as he kept calling me Molly when my name is Mary, and then one day he explained he is afflicted with lambdacism.

∾

Lambent: Derived from the Latin word *lambere*, meaning to lick. Lambent describes something flickering or moving smoothly or lightly over a surface or something shining softly and brightly. The word is also often associated with light and exquisiteness of expression in writing.

'Those smiling eyes, attemp'ring ev'ry ray,
Shone sweetly lambent with celestial day.'

Alexander Pope, *Eloisa to Abelard* (1717)

∾

Lamentable: The original meaning of lamentable was that which is sorrowful and grief inducing – such as a funeral service. Over time, however, it has come to be used to describe anything that is pitiful and pathetic. It is unclear exactly when this shift in meaning came about but it was possibly due to Victorian attitudes to expressions of weakness and being stoic in the face of adversity.

All in all it was a lamentable attempt at fixing the washing machine, which resulted in flooding the whole flat.

∾

Lampadedromy and Lampadophory: In Ancient Greece a *lampadedromy* was a race in which participants carried a lighted torch and handed it, as in a relay, to other participants. The modern Olympics enacts an extended lampadedromy when passing the Olympic flame from one host country to the next. Lampadophory is a figurative and metaphorical noun for the passing on of an idea from one generation to the next – the torchbearer for human rights and equality.

After Mandela retired there was an absence of lampadophory in finding a successor to carry on the programme of reform in South Africa.

∾

Lancination: From the Latin word to lacerate, *lancinare*, lancination describes a sharp shooting or piercing pain in a part of the body.

Hemi-cranial headaches are sharp lancinations behind one eye and across the side of the head.

∾

Languor and Languid: Languor is a feeling of listlessness or inertia, often brought on by weariness of the body or the mind. As an adjectival form, though, languid is much more positive, suggesting a certain lazy and idle charm in manner.

Goncharov's languid prose style is befitting of the subject matter in his masterpiece Oblomov.

∾

Laniate: In Latin *lanius* is the word for butcher and so when we laniate something we butcher it by ripping it to pieces.

I laniated the letter I received from the council and flushed the pieces down the toilet.

∾

Lapidate and Lapidation: To lapidate is to pelt somebody with stones. Death by lapidation was common in the Middle Ages and is still sanctioned by law in some countries of the world, although rarely carried out.

The lapidation scene in Monty Python's Life of Brian *is a comedy classic.*

∾

Largesse: *Largesse* in Middle English meant, more or less, largeness. The word has come to be associated with the liberal giving of money, often ostentatiously, to people or causes.

Henry Ford was not a natural philanthropist but was given to public displays of charitable largesse.

~

Larine: Larine is specific to gulls (not terns) and is anything pertaining to, resembling or associated with this species of sea bird.

I'm woken every morning by the larine calling of the birds outside my window.

~

Larrikin: An Australian English word, larrikin was originally a term for a rowdy and loutish young man with little respect for authority. In recent times, however, there has been much debate about the 'larrikin streak' in Australian culture, which roughly translates as being boorish and wilfully uncultured as an antidote to British imperial manners and attitudes.

The larrikin streak in Australians is epitomized by the behaviour of their sports teams.

~

Lassitude: A state of weariness and general apathy. Often used as a medical word for exhaustion, lassitude is also used in a figurative sense to describe something that is negligent and 'on its last legs'.

The government was faltering under the weight of failed policies and economic lassitude.

~

Latebricole: An odd word derived from the French *latebricola*, which meant somebody who lives in hiding. Latebricole in English is used in zoology to describe creatures that live inside concealed holes.

The common house spider is an example of a latebricole creature.

~

Latitant: Latitant is another word concerning concealment, possibly somebody hiding away for some reason (personal safety or evading criminal prosecution). Latitant in zoology relates to any animal that hibernates in the winter.

Hedgehogs are latitant animals that hibernate every year.

~

Latitudinarian and Latitudinous: The world would perhaps be a better place with more latitudinarians. The word relates to a person who does not follow or insist on conforming to any particular doctrine or code but preaches tolerance of any opinions, religious and political. The adjective latitudinous relates to a sense of tolerance but can also mean to give a broad and wide interpretation of something that is deliberately not rigid but flexible.

There was some concern within the Roman Catholic hierarchy that the new Pope may be a little too latitudinarian in his attitude to other religions.

~

Latria: In Roman Catholicism latria is the word for the homage and service given to God (worship). The word derives from the Greek word *látris*, meaning servant, and it is this sense of servitude before the Lord Almighty that pervades the meaning of latria.

Hyperdulia is veneration reserved for the Virgin alone; and latria is given to God and to each person of the Trinity.

~

Laudatory: Any language, written or spoken, that expresses praise is laudatory. The Latin word *laudare* means to applaud and that is essentially what laudatory does, but with words rather than hands.

He delivered a laudatory speech.

~

Lavation: The Latin word *lavare*, meaning to wash, provides the root for several words in English ranging from lavish (which originally in Middle French meant a torrential downpour) to lavatory. The act of lavation, however, is simply washing or cleansing.

After five days camping I was desperately in need of some lavation.

~

Lazaret: Borrowed from the Italian word *lazaretto*, a lazaret is a hospital for patients with terminal or highly contagious diseases, particularly leprosy in the Middle Ages.

We visited the church of Santa Maria di Nazareth in Venice, which at one time acted as a lazaret for lepers.

~

Lebensraum: In German *leben* means living and *raum* means space, so strictly speaking lebensraum means living space. The word, however, was adopted by the Nazis as a slogan promoting an agrarian (and sinister) view of the essentials needed for life, growth and vitality.

The Nazis had various ideological words that they adopted, and lebensraum was one of the key concepts.

~

Leiotrichous and Lissotrichous: A pair of elaborate words to describe straight (leiotrichous) or smooth and soft (lissotrichous) hair.

She ran her fingers through her dark, leiotrichous, hair.

~

Lendrumbilate: An obscure word, which is possibly a hoax as it appears in few dictionaries, but (allegedly) to lendrumbilate is to gullibly believe in the truth behind the meaning of a word.

It is to be hoped that no readers of this book will be required to lendrumbilate.

~

Lenify, Lenitive and Lenity: From the Latin word for soft, *lenis*, comes a lovely calming string of words. To lenify is to assuage or calm something or someone. Similarly, a lenitive action, such as taking a nice warm bath, can ease aches and pains. Finally, lenity is the quality of being kind and gentle.

My father exudes such lenity in the manner in which he deals with difficult people.

~

Lentitude: In contrast to the previous entry, lentitude has a thoroughly different meaning and relates to sluggishness and indolence.

My teenage daughter exhibits lentitude bordering upon contempt when told to clean up her bedroom.

~

Lepid: An archaic word that doesn't really convey what it means. A lepid comment or remark is one that is amusing or funny in a light-hearted way and yet it sounds as if it should mean the opposite.

She broke the ice with her boyfriend's parents by making a couple of lepid remarks over lunch.

~

Lethe and Lethonomia: In Greek mythology the river Lethe is in Hades, the underworld, and drinking its waters causes people to forget their past sins and misdemeanours and enter into a state of oblivion. Lethe in English is an old-fashioned word for forgetfulness. Lethonomia is the inability to remember names.

I suffer bouts of lethonomia at parties when it comes to remembering people's names.

~

Lethiferous: Anything that is lethiferous is lethal and will kill you, be it a substance, agent or situation.

He poisoned his wife by pouring lethiferous liquids into her coffee.

~

Lexicology: Lexicology is a branch of linguistics specifically focused on the meaning and application of words.

It is hoped this book may make a contribution to the field of lexicology.

~

Lexiphanic: Lexiphanic describes a person who uses ostentatiously long words when speaking, essentially to show off their learning or to intimidate and confuse. *Lexiphanes* was an essay by the Ancient Greek satirist and rhetorician Lucian of Samosata (AD 125–80). The essay takes the form of a dialogue between Lucian and an extremely pompous man called Lexiphanes who tries to befuddle Lucian with long words.

It's okay to strive to improve your vocabulary but be careful of cultivating lexiphanic tendencies.

~

Libertinage: The actions and practices of a libertine – a person who wilfully cultivates a disregard for moral instruction in social, sexual or religious matters in search of personal pleasure.

Les Liaisons dangereuses (Dangerous Liaisons, 1782), an epistolary novel by Pierre Choderlos de Laclos, is a trenchant description of sexual libertinage in eighteenth-century France.

~

Libidinous: A libidinous person is driven by the desires of their libido and seeks lustful and sensual excitement. The word libido is a fairly recent borrowing into English and is thought to have been first coined at the turn of the twentieth century by Sigmund Freud.

The novel concerns the libidinous lifestyle of a lawyer and his masochistic sexual endeavours.

~

Licentious: Licentious behaviour means lacking legal or moral restraints and is often related to matters of sexuality. The word derives from the Latin noun *licentia*, the meanings of which range from freedom to act, to unruly behaviour and wantonness.

> *The licentious and corrupt culture of the Roman Empire ultimately led to its decline.*

∽

Lickerish: Lickerish is a word that has gone full circle in terms of meaning. In the fourteenth century, the adjective lickerous meant a person who lived a debauched lifestyle. The word derived from the French *lecher* (from where we also get lecherous) but had a secondary meaning of to lick or taste something with the tongue. By the seventeenth century lickerish had come to mean somebody with an appetite for good food. Over time this food-related meaning developed to denote somebody who was greedy and wanton in satisfying their desires (interestingly, this is the meaning that prevails in West Indian English/Patois today). Eventually, this overtly desirous meaning came to be attached again to matters of the flesh, and lickerish has once more become a synonym for being lecherous.

> *'Shall we go back to my place?' he said with a lustful, lickerish grin.*

∽

Ligneous, Ligniform and Lignify: The Latin word for wood – *lignum* – is responsible for several rare words in English. Something ligneous is made of wood or wooden in aspect. Something ligniform has the appearance of wood but is artificial and made from wood-like materials. The verb to lignify in biological terms is to turn into wood through the insertion of lignins, a natural polymer, into the cell walls of plants.

> *I was disappointed with the tree I planted from a seedling as at first it appeared to be little more than a shrub – over time, however, the trunk began to lignify and turn brown and rigid.*

∽

Lineament: A lineament is most commonly a distinctive feature, contour or shape of a body or figure, and especially faces. It is sometimes figuratively used to describe general characteristics of something or someone; for example, the lineaments of a company's advertising campaign. In geology, lineaments are topographical features on or below the earth's surface, such as fault lines.

The lineaments of his face were very expressive, especially when he laughed or smiled.

~

Lissom: Lissom is an alteration of the much older word lithesome (from the Old English *lithe*, meaning gentle). Lissom in particular relates to the body being supple and nimble in movement. The word is sometimes spelt lissome.

The lissom actor's background training in classical ballet showed from the graceful manner in which she glides across the stage.

~

Literal versus Littoral: Literal derives from the Latin word for letter, *littera*. A literal reading of something adheres to the primary and basic meaning, free from exaggeration or embellishment. A littoral area relates to lakes and oceans and describes the region around the shoreline.

The story he told was basically true, even if it wasn't the literal truth.

~

Litotes: Derived from the Greek word *litos*, meaning simple, litotes is a rhetorical term for defining something by affirming its opposite. Pedantic grammarians often decry litotes as being examples of double negatives but it's *not unusual* to find it in all forms of speech and writing. Litotes is particularly common in poetry, where it is often used for ironic understatement.

It was not uncommon to find him lurking at the water cooler at lunchtime.

~

Loath versus Loathe versus Loathsome: When we are loath to do something it is because it is contrary to our way of thinking or point of view, so we are reluctant to change our minds. When we loathe something it is because we detest it and find it has a loathsome aspect which we feel strongly about. Loathsome, interestingly, derives from the Middle English word *lothsum*, meaning evil and disgusting.

He was loath to change his mind once he'd made a decision.

I absolutely loathe television talent shows.

He was a truly loathsome individual with vile habits.

∽

Locution: Locution relates to a particular quality of expression or phrasing in speech or writing and especially of a certain region, group or culture.

Often written in the vernacular and locution of his Deep South protagonists, the novels of William Faulkner can be difficult for readers unaccustomed to his style.

∽

Lodestar: The original meaning of lodestar was a star that can used to lead or guide, such as the star of Bethlehem in Bible mythology or the North Star for travellers. A figurative sense emerged of a lodestar as a bright, shining inspiration or model.

It is sobering to think that consumerism, selfishness and greed are the primary lodestars of modern civilization.

∽

Longanimity: Longanimity has been in English since the mid-fifteenth century and derives from the Middle French word *longanimité*, meaning patience. To have the capacity for loganimity means to exhibit forbearance of misfortune, especially in unfortunate circumstances such as long-term illness or injury.

She displayed terrific courage and longanimity during long periods of convalescence by maintaining a cheery and optimistic disposition.

∽

Longevity: Deriving from the Latin *longaevus* (*longus* meaning long and *aevum* meaning age) and first recorded in the English language in 1569, longevity is a long length of life or a continuous period of time relating to an activity or state.

No one was surprised that Grandma had reached 100 as there was a history of longevity on the female side of her family.

~

Loquacious: From the Latin word to speak – *loqui* – loquacious means to be excessively chatty and garrulous. The word appears in seventeenth- and eighteenth-century nature poetry in a figurative sense, describing everything from the sounds of bird song to bubbling brooks, but in its strictest sense it means somebody who maybe talks too much.

The loquacious style of Talk Radio presenters gets on my nerves.

~

Louche: The Latin word for being blind in one eye or poor of sight was *luscus*. The French developed this word into *louche*, which originally described somebody cross-eyed or squinting. A figurative meaning developed that people who squinted were not to be trusted and were dishonest or of ill repute. Louche entered into the English language in the nineteenth century and retains the French meaning of somebody who is shady or indecent in manner or action. It is also used of places where louche activities take place.

The Late Night Diner is full of louche characters.

~

Lucubration: Lucubrations are painstaking, laborious and intense periods of study or the product of such endeavours. The word derives from the Latin word *lucubrare*, meaning to study by lamp or candlelight, and is redolent of working through the night.

My final term at university involved many evenings of lucubration writing my dissertation.

~

Luculent: The Latin word *lux* means light. Something luculent was originally a description of something shining or emitting light, such as a candle flame. By the mid-sixteenth century the word became closely related to lucid and developed the sense of clarity of thought or expression.

The lawyer's luculent closing observations swayed the jury.

∽

Lugubrious: Lugubrious describes someone or something mournful and sorrowful in manner or disposition. Lugubrious people are prone to brooding and maintain, often for effect, a negative and downbeat disposition. Lugubrious can also be applied to music and art, such as the mournful laments in the poetry of Edgar Allan Poe.

The lugubrious style of the songs of Leonard Cohen is not to everyone's taste.

∽

Lutaceous and Lutarious: Both words are derived from the Latin word *lutum*, meaning mud. Lutaceous is something comprised or made of mud or having the texture of mud. Lutarious relates to something that lives in mud and swamps.

Hippos undertake their lutarious lounging during periods of extreme heat, as the mud protects their fragile skin.

∽

Lycanthropy: Derived from the Greek words *lykos*, meaning wolf, and *anthropos*, meaning human being, lycanthropy is the delusion of or belief in human beings turning into werewolves.

Stories and myths of lycanthropy are prevalent in many different cultures.

M

Mabble: The verb to mabble means to wrap something up, usually a gift. The origin of the word is uncertain but it possibly comes from the tradition of wrapping up flowers in little woven baskets to celebrate May Day.

I don't usually mabble my Christmas presents until Christmas Eve.

Macarize: To macarize is to laud somebody or to pronounce them happy or blessed. The earliest usage of the word is found in the writings of Richard Whately (1787–1863), the Church of Ireland Archbishop of Dublin, theologian and philosopher.

The wedding was suitably celebratory, with the happy couple macarized in the usual fashion by the priest.

Macaroni: Small slender tubes of pasta don't warrant an entry in this book, but the secondary meaning of a macaroni as the disparaging term for a dandyish fop of independent means does. In the 1760s a gentlemen's club sprang up in London comprised of rich, fashionable young men who had taken Grand Tours of Europe and affected continental mannerisms. The club was called The Macaroni Club, presumably because they thought small slender tubes of pasta to be the height of sophistication at the time.

The life of a macaroni centred on elaborate dressing habits and endless upper-class social engagements.

Macerate and Macilent: Macerate is derived from the Latin verb *macerare*, meaning to soften or to steep by soaking in liquid (often alcohol when making fruit liquors). An older meaning for macerate concerned wasting away due to fasting, starvation or ill-health. This later meaning, although very rare, has become superseded by emaciate, of which macilent is a synonym meaning excessively thin.

Cherry brandy is easy to make at home: macerate fresh cherries in sugar and alcohol and leave for the flavour to infuse.

He arrived at the party accompanied by his pale, macilent daughter.

~

Machiavellian: This word is named after Niccolò Machiavelli (1469–1527), an Italian political philosopher whose work *The Prince* earned him a reputation as an atheist and an immoral cynic. Its first known use as a derogatory term was in 1572, and it is now used to describe behaviour that is cunning, duplicitous or in bad faith.

The leader of the council displayed Machiavellian traits.

~

Macrocephalous: The scientific term to describe a species or person with an enormous or abnormally large head.

My parents were concerned by my macrocephalous appearance when I was a baby and took me to the hospital for tests.

~

Maculate: Maculate has been in English since the fourteenth century and derives from the Latin *maculare*, meaning to stain or blemish. Around the time the word first appeared, spots, blemishes or lesions on the skin were among the symptoms of the Black Death, so for someone to become spotted (maculated) was usually very bad news.

Among Damien Hirst's first big hits in the art world were his maculate coloured compositions called The Spot Paintings.

~

Maffick: To maffick is to celebrate something with boisterous abandon. The word derives from the Boer War and the Siege of Mafeking, a battle in which the British Army, although outnumbered, managed to hold firm for 217 days. When news of the significant victory on 17 May 1900 filtered through to Britain it sparked wild celebrations in towns and cities.

There was much mafficking in major cities when England won the football World Cup.

~

Magniloquent: *Magnus* in Latin means great and *loqui* was the verb for to speak – thus magniloquent is to speak in a high-blown and often bombastic manner. Grandiloquent is a direct synonym but there is no difference in meaning other than that *grandis* is the Latin word for grand.

He delivered his speech in his usual magniloquent manner.

~

Maieutic: *Maieutikos* in Greek means the practice of midwifery and this rarely seen word in English is used to describe the study and training given to midwives. It also has a much older meaning courtesy of the Ancient Greek philosopher Socrates, who used maieutic to describe his process of developing ideas through reason and dialogue (the so-called Socratic Method). Socrates used midwifery as a metaphor for giving birth to ideas that were already latent inside people. It should come as no surprise that Socrates' mother was a midwife.

We engaged in maieutic exchanges at Philosophy Club on the nature versus nurture debate.

~

Maladroit: In Middle French, *maladroit* was used to refer to people who were clumsy or accident prone. *Droit* is a direction in French meaning straight or right, so maladroit literally means 'badly straight' or 'not right'; the assumption is that clumsy people have a habit of bumping into things. By the seventeenth century, English borrowed the word but added a wider context of someone being inept and incompetent.

The government has faced criticism for its maladroit handling of trade negotiations.

Malapert: Malapert is formed by the prefix *mal*, meaning bad, and the Middle English word *apert*, meaning open. The word describes people who are bold and boisterous but in an often negative or detrimental way – literally 'badly open' or impudent. Shakespeare was particularly fond of the word, as the following quote from a slighted Sir Toby Belch in *Twelfth Night* illustrates:

'What, what? Nay, then I must have an ounce or two of this malapert blood from you.'

William Shakespeare, *Twelfth Night*, Act 4, Scene 1

Malapropism: A malapropism is an unintentional confusion of one word for another usually similar-sounding word to produce comic effect. The word takes its name from Mrs Malaprop, a character in Richard Sheridan's 1775 play *The Rivals*, who was known for her verbal blunders, examples of which are highlighted in the quote below:

'I would have her instructed in geometry, that she might know something of the contagious countries;—but above all, Sir Anthony, she should be mistress of orthodoxy, that she might not misspell, and mis-pronounce words so shamefully as girls usually do; and likewise that she might reprehend the true meaning of what she is saying.'

Richard Sheridan, *The Rivals*, Act 1, Scene 2

Malediction: The word malediction derives from the Latin *maledicere*, meaning to speak badly of or to speak evil of. The word at one time merely related to being socially slandered or reviled, but this meaning has more or less disappeared and now a malediction is basically a curse directed at someone or something.

The beggar walked off muttering maledictions when I waved away her request for money.

Malfeasance: A technical term often applied to politicians or people in positions of power and responsibility, malfeasance means intentional wrong-doing or illegal activities.

Several large corporations are the subject of investigations into malfeasance in their corporate tax payments.

~

Malinger: The verb to malinger comes from the French word for sickly, *malinger*, and means to fake illness to avoid work or duty. The word first appeared in English in the 1820s at the height of the Industrial Revolution, which was probably around the time people initially started calling in sick to shirk work.

My friend was caught out malingering when her boss checked her Facebook updates.

~

Malodorous: Something malodorous is usually something that smells bad. Another word stemming from the Latin *mal*, malodorous can also be used in a more generalized way for something that stinks in a metaphorical sense.

Despite all attempts to cover up the details and brush things under the carpet, the whole affair was malodorous.

~

Mammon and Mammonism: Mammon is an archaic word that originally entered into English from Greek via the Aramaic languages (*māmōnā*) in the fifteenth century. Essentially, mammon is material wealth and possessions, and it is seen in theology as having potentially a corrupting or debasing influence on spiritual well-being. By extension, mammonism is the greedy and almost pathological pursuit of wealth and riches.

You cannot serve God and mammon.

The Bible, Matthew 6:24

~

Manège: A direct borrowing from the French *manège*, this denotes the art of horsemanship or the art of training horses.

A master in the technicalities of manège, French trainer André Fabre has a worldwide reputation in the sport of horse racing.

~

Manifest: Manifest derives from the Latin *manifestus* – to be caught in the act, flagrant, obvious – and has been used in the English language since the fourteenth century. It has come to describe something easily understood, seen to be evident.

The actor playing the psychopath succeeded in manifesting a sense of true evil.

~

Manifold: Manifold means many or varied and diverse. In a positive sense it could describe the manifold delights of the city of Barcelona. In a negative sense (in which it is often used) it could describe the manifold issues or problems someone has encountered. The word was once used as a verb to describe making multiple copies of a book.

There are manifold issues with the trade negotiations.

~

Manner, Mannered, Mannerly and Mannerism: Manner initially described a type or sort but quickly became a way in which something is done or occurs. This sense of the manner in which we behave developed into adjective forms, either well-mannered or ill-mannered, or as a rather elegant character trait, mannerly, meaning polite. The word mannered also began to be used to describe actors delivering a mannered performance (as in the style of). Finally, all this play acting must have paid off because the noun mannerism arrived in English to describe characteristic and often unconscious modes of behaviour, such as verbal impediments or facial tics.

He was an excellent mimic and could impersonate people's mannerisms to great effect.

~

Manqué: This is a curious adjective etymologically, as the word is a hybrid of French word *manqué*, meaning to fail or be unfulfilled, and the Italian word *manco*, meaning having a crippled hand or being left-handed. Although remaining true to its original meaning of failure or lacking, the word manqué has a positive sense of something as yet to be fulfilled in terms of ambition and aspirations.

I've always thought of myself as very much a romancier manqué (frustrated novelist), as the French would say.

∼

Mansuetude: Mansuetude first appeared in English in the fourteenth century, and derives from the Latin verb *mansuescere*, which means to tame. *Mansuescere* is formed by the noun *manus*, meaning hand, and the verb *suescere*, which means to become accustomed. A modern description of the Latin word would be 'brought to hand'. Mansuetude is therefore the quality of being meek, tame or gentle.

It took some time to train my dog but now he has mansuetude and no longer urinates on the kitchen floor.

∼

Manumission: Manumission is the process or act of individuals or groups receiving emancipation and freedom from slavery.

The official manumission of the slaves in the United States came only after the Civil War.

∼

Maricolous, Marigenous and Mariculture: The Latin word for the sea, *mare*, has provided several adjectives which, rather sadly, have all been eclipsed by the generalized term maritime. To be specific, maricolous means things that live in the sea. Marigenous is something produced in or by the sea. A mariculture denotes sub-aquatic plants and fauna that form ecosystems such as kelp forests and coral reefs.

In the future it may be possible to cheaply harness marigenous power sources.

~

Marplot and Mar-joy: The prefix *mar*, meaning to spoil, developed in English in the seventeenth century. Marplot became the name for someone who spoils a plan by interfering; similarly a mar-joy was somebody who spoils other people's fun or good humour – a forerunner of the modern term killjoy.

> *"'What does all this mean?' asked Charles, in the darkness, in a tone which was beginning to betray a formidable accent of impatience. 'Am I such a mar-joy that the sight of me causes all this confusion?'"*
>
> Alexandre Dumas, *Queen Margot* (1845)

~

Martinet: The term martinet describes a person who is a strict disciplinarian, hard taskmaster and stickler for the rules. The word comes from the name of the stern seventeenth-century French soldier, Lieutenant Colonel John Martinet, who served Louis XIV and was famous for his obsessive marshalling of his troops.

> *My father was very laid-back when I was growing up and seemed determined not to be a martinet like his father was to him.*

~

Masquerade: A masquerade was originally a lavish social gathering of persons wearing masks and often fantastic costumes attended by courtiers and aristocrats. Over time the word developed into a verb form to mean pretending to be somebody else or to put on a disguise.

> *Shakespeare's comedies often centre upon characters masquerading as somebody else.*

~

Masticate: Derived from Latin via the Greek *mastichan*, this means to gnash or grind the teeth. To masticate in polite company isn't always pleasant for other people to see. The word is often, for example, used in relation to cows, which excessively chew grass in order to digest it properly.

His eating habits are atrocious; watching him masticate on a baguette turns my stomach.

~

Mathesis: An archaic word derived from the Greek word *mathēsis*, meaning the acquisition of knowledge or the moment of knowing or understanding. The word is also linked to mathematics, for the Greeks didn't distinguish between the different physical sciences and philosophy, so all knowledge or *mathēsis* was interlinked.

No process of mathesis is without some value.

~

Matriarch: Matriarch is often used in a slightly pejorative way to describe a mother or grandmother who dominates a large family and has power and influence over its members.

My grandmother loved to play the matriarch at family gatherings.

~

Maudlin: Mary Magdalene was, according to the Bible, a fallen woman who washed the feet of Jesus with her tears, and it is from her name that the word maudlin is derived. The early Bible translations into English spelt Mary's name as Mary Maudelayne. Over time this spelling, during the period of the Great Vowel Shift (the evolution of the pronunciation of English vowel sounds between the fourteenth and sixteenth centuries), gave birth to the word maudlin to mean tearful or sorrowful. This is also the reason why Magdalene College Cambridge and Magdalen College Oxford are pronounced 'maudlin'.

I can't drink gin; it makes me maudlin and depressed.

~

Maunder versus Meander: Maunder is a word that causes some confusion due to its close proximity in meaning to 'meander'. The actual derivation of the word is unclear, which accounts in part for the lack of clarity in its definition, but perhaps that is the point. For the sake of argument, people meander aimlessly around in physical terms but maunder when speaking with a lack of focus or lucidity. Maunder is also sometimes used to describe a person grumbling or moaning.

I asked her a simple question and she maundered on and on without giving me an answer.

~

Mausoleum: The Mausoleum at Halicarnassus was a lavishly decorated tomb built in honour of Mausolus, a governor of the Persian Empire around AD 350. Considered as one of the Seven Wonders of the Ancient World, the Mausoleum was destroyed by earthquakes in the twelfth and fifteenth centuries. The word mausoleum derives from the legendary structure and means any lavish or extravagant, above-ground, tomb.

It's a symbol of utmost opulence and arrogance to construct your own mausoleum prior to death.

~

Mediate: To mediate is to act as a moderator between two opposing factions in an argument or a dispute to try and reconcile differences. The noun form mediate is the middle point on a scale or a graph.

I was called upon to mediate between two colleagues who had long-standing grievances with each other.

~

Megrim: The Middle English word *migreime* was borrowed from the French *migraine*, which is the same in meaning as the contemporary word for hemi-cranial pains and dizziness. However, in the Middle Ages megrim had a slightly different meaning, often relating to psychological moments such as random thoughts, flights of fancy or even hallucinations. During the Middle Ages there were frequent outbreaks of ergotism – poisoning by eating grain infested with a powerful fungus. Among the symptoms of ergotism were extreme headaches, mania and hallucinations, which were known as megrims.

Since turning fifty my brother seems to have become afflicted with the megrims; he keeps coming up with wild plans for things he wants to do.

~

Mellifluous versus Melliferous: Although both words derive from the Latin word for honey, *mel*, there is a difference in usage. Mellifluous means something that flows smoothly and sweetly and is often applied to sounds, especially music and voices. Melliferous describes something that produces honey or is made with honey.

> *'Wisest of men; from whose mouth issu'd forth Mellifluous streams.'*
>
> John Milton, *Paradise Regained* (1671)

∾

Mendacious: A word that is perhaps not as uncommon in present times as it once was. To make a mendacious statement or indulge in mendacities is to wilfully tell lies and utter untruths.

> *The development of the internet and mass media has led some social and political commentators to claim we live in an era of 'post-truth' and 'fake news' where organizations, individuals and institutions are mendacious and not to be trusted.*

∾

Mendicancy: Derived from the Old French *mendicité*, meaning begging, mendicancy is the state or practice of depending on alms and handouts in order to live.

> *Mendicancy is so rife on the streets of our towns and cities.*

∾

Mercurial: Mercury was the Roman messenger god who was revered for his cunning, eloquence and swiftness of thought and deed. Originally, the word mercurial meant born under the sign of Mercury, but over time the adjective evolved to describe characteristics in keeping with the god Mercury, namely sharpness or mind, ingenuity and even deviousness (Mercury was also the god of thieves). A modern usage of mercurial is also to describe somebody changeable in actions and temperament.

> *My sister has a mercurial mind, always jumping from one thought to the next; it's exhausting talking to her.*

~

Meretricious: An archaic adjective with several different meanings and uses. The original Latin word *meretricius* was used to describe the appearance, demeanour and behaviour of a prostitute. Although this meaning still survives in modern usage, most commonly in legal language ('the defendant had several meretricious relationships with women during his marriage, your honour') the meaning of the word has broadened. Meretricious can also be used to describe the appearance of something that appears to be attractive and expensive but is actually very cheap and nasty and/or something that is garish and gaudy.

The hotel lobby has a meretricious interior décor designed in a dishonest attempt to attract a better class of customer.

~

Meronym: Meronym is a semantic term for a word used to describe relationships between lexical items. Meronyms are groups of words that are linked conceptually, for example wall is a meronym of house. Meronyms are also defined as either necessary or obligatory. Wall is a necessary meronym of house as all houses have walls. Window, however, is an obligatory meronym of house, as not all houses have windows.

Branch is a necessary meronym of tree.

~

Metanoia: From the Greek word *metanoiein*, meaning to change one's mind, metanoia expressly refers to undergoing some sort of spiritual conversion, often as a form of repentance.

When my cousin returned from travelling in Asia he underwent a metanoiac conversion to Buddhism.

~

Metensomatosis versus Metempsychosis: In biology, metensomatosis is the process whereby one body or organism assimilates elements of another, thereby creating a hybrid organism.

Metempsychosis is the belief that the soul transmigrates from the body after death into a new body, either of the same or of a different species.

If metempsychosis is real, I'd like to come back to life as a cat.

~

Methomania and Methysis: Words related to drinking alcohol include methomania – a morbid pathological craving for alcohol – distinct from dipsomania, which is a pathological need to be drunk or to experience methysis (an archaic word for drunkenness).

When I gave up alcohol on medical grounds, despite years of heavy drinking I experienced few feelings of methomania.

~

Metonym: A word that is used as a substitute for something with which it is closely related. For example: Westminster, although an area of London, is frequently used as a byword for the British government and, in particular, the Houses of Parliament.

The Kremlin is a metonym for the Russian government.

~

Miasma: Derived from the Greek word *miainein*, meaning to pollute, a miasma was originally a foul-smelling vapour emitted by decaying matter that was thought to spread diseases and ill-health. The more modern figurative sense of miasma is of something decaying and polluting that has formed a metaphorical cloud of stench.

A miasma of sexual harassment is lingering over Hollywood after recent allegations.

~

Micawber: A micawber is a person of modest income or background who nonetheless remains optimistic that their situation will improve, and is named after the character Wilkins Micawber in Charles Dickens' novel *David Copperfield* (1850). In the novel,

Micawber suffers great hardship but remains optimistic and faithful to his mantra that 'something will turn up'.

My grandfather was something of a micawber, never letting setbacks or misfortune drag down his cheery disposition.

∽

Militate and Mitigate: In American English there is much confusion over the difference between the verbs militate and mitigate. The former (militate) means to apply pressure or force against something to affect it in some way. To mitigate is to lessen the impact of something or to cause it to become less harsh or hostile and make a situation less severe or painful.

He didn't get the job, but felt, in mitigation, that his age had militated against him.

∽

Mordant: An often misunderstood and misused word, mordant has nothing to do with being morbid or excessively gloomy in outlook. To have a mordant sense of humour is to display the ability to make cutting and caustic comments and jokes in social situations. A mordant is also the technical term for the substance used to fix coloured dyes on to fabrics and textiles.

Oscar Wilde was famous for his mordant quips and ripostes.

∽

Myopic: First used in 1800, myopia is a medical term for near-sightedness. However, the adjective is also often used to describe someone, or some policy, lacking in foresight, with a narrow perspective and little concern for the broader implications.

The talk-show host has a myopic viewpoint and is never willing to listen to his guests' perspectives.

∽

Myriad: Myriad actually means ten thousand but is often used to denote, generally, a great number. It has been used in the English language since the sixteenth century and comes from the Greek *myrias*, which means countless or ten thousand.

There are a myriad of stars in the Milky Way.

N

~

Nacreous: An odd adjective that relates entirely to the translucent light produced by mother-of-pearl accoutrements (buttons, badges etc.) on garments or jewellery.

The suit was divine, the nacreous buttons shone and sparkled in the sunlight.

~

Nadir: Nadir derives from an Arabic word meaning opposite – the opposite, that is, of the zenith, which means the highest point you can achieve (or in astrology the highest point in the sky). To reach one's zenith, metaphorically, means reaching a pinnacle; to slump to one's nadir is to have slipped as low as it's possible to go.

We reached our nadir as a team when we lost every match for two years in a row.

~

Napifolious and Napifolic: It is pretty hard to believe but there are adjectives for a plant as humble as the turnip. Napifolious means to have flowering leaves like a turnip – napifolic means to have the characteristics of a turnip.

I'm not a fan of root vegetables but love the napifolious flowers they sprout.

~

Narrowback: A term, often used disparagingly, to describe first-generation Irish Americans. The word is frequently also used to describe somebody of slight build who is not fit for manual labouring tasks.

My ancestors emigrated to America in the 1840s so I am descended from several generations of narrowbacks.

∾

Nasallate: Nasallate describes a low, stuffy tone of voice, also called a nasally voice.

The bank clerk had a gruff nasallate voice that made him hard to understand.

∾

Nascent: Derived from the Latin verb *nasci*, meaning to be born, nascent describes something that has recently come into existence or is in its early stages of development. The word is often used to describe companies and organizations.

The nascent electric car industry requires careful and sustained investment in order for it to grow.

∾

Natation and Natatorium: The Latin word for swimming is *natāre* and this provides the stem for natation – an old-fashioned word for the art or technique of swimming. A natatorium is a slightly pretentious word for an indoor swimming pool.

The hotel brochure listed a natatorium among its facilities.

∾

Naufrage and Naufrageous: A naufrage is a nautical term for a shipwreck. Although rarely used outside of maritime circles, naufrage has given rise to the adjective naufrageous, which can be used figuratively to describe something going to rack and ruin or in danger of being destroyed.

The lack of proper infrastructure meant future developments and plans were in a naufrageous position.

~

Nebulous: *Nebula* is the Latin word for mist or fog. The word is used in astronomy to describe celestial objects such as clouds of gas and dust particles in space and/or galaxies. The original Latin sense of fog or mist informs the adjective nebulous, which is used, often negatively, to describe something indistinct or not clearly formed.

I have only very nebulous memories of my childhood.

~

Necrology: A word that sounds as if it should mean the study of death but is actually an alternative term for an obituary or eulogy.

The priest delivered an extensive necrology detailing the deceased's life and achievements.

~

Necrophagous, Necrophobia and Necromancy: The Greek word for a dead body/person, *nekrós* has given rise to many words beginning with the suffix *necro*. Necrophagous describes an organism that feeds on the carrion and corpses of other animals. Necrophobia is a fear of seeing or discovering a dead body. Necromancy is a form of black magic in which communication is made with the spirits of the dead, usually to predict or influence future events.

The corpse of the zebra had been picked clean by necrophagous insects and buzzards.

Many women were burned at the stake after accusations of practising necromancy.

~

Nefandous and Nefarious: In the sixteenth century the Latin word *nefās* was largely a legal term that related to committing an offence against religious or moral law. This gave rise to the adjectives nefandous and nefarious, both of which relate to wicked and despicable deeds. The slight difference in the meaning of the two words is that the less commonly used nefandous means unspeakable acts, whereas nefarious is just generally doing bad things.

The State Department has pledged to crack down on the nefarious activities of drug cartels.

∾

Négociant: A *négociant* is a French term, borrowed into English, to describe a wine merchant. Specifically a *négociant* buys up grape stocks and wines from smaller producers and repackages them for resale under a different brand or house.

Burgundy's fragmented nature means négociants are the region's glue – and sources of great value.

∾

Neologism: A neologism (from Greek *neo*, meaning new, and *logos*, meaning speech) is a new word coinage, usually a word that is in common usage but that has not been formally recognized as being part of the language in question.

The explosion in information technology in the 1990s gave rise to a rush of neologisms that are now part of everyday language.

∾

Neophyte: The Latin word *neophytus* originally meant newly planted. The term neophyte initially related to the Catholic Church, novice monks being known as neophytes. This led in turn to the word becoming generally used to mean a recent convert to a religion or faith and, by extension, someone new or unaccustomed to something.

I'm a neophyte with computers, I can only just about turn them on.

∾

Nepenthe: In ancient times a nepenthe was a mythical drink or substance that helped the poor to find relief or forgetfulness from sorrow or grief – a sort of proto-anti-depressant. The term can also be used generally to describe something that causes us to forget our troubles and woes.

He often used alcohol as a crutch and a nepenthe when feeling down.

~

Nervine: Nervines are usually plant or natural remedies, common in holistic medicine, that are used to calm the nerves by acting as sedatives.

I struggled with the medicine I had been prescribed so my doctor suggested trying nervine remedies.

~

Nescience: The Latin verb *scire* means to know and from this, when combined with a negative prefix, we get the word nescience, which means to be ignorant and lack knowledge (to 'not know').

My nescience of foreign languages is a cause of embarrassment to me when I travel abroad.

~

Nictate: To nictate is the technical term for winking or blinking or pressing the eyelids together.

Her eyes began to nictate rapidly, betraying signs of anxiety.

~

Nidget: Derived from the Old French word *niger*, meaning to play the fool, a nidget is an archaic word for an idiot and clown or somebody who is foolish and cowardly.

There are some great insults in Old English like fopdoodle and nidget.

~

Nimiety: Roughly synonymous with superfluous, nimiety derives from *nimius*, the Latin word for too much or excessive.

The nimiety of Christmas decorations draped over every possible part of the room represented something of a fire hazard.

~

Nitency: Nitency has two meanings, as it is derived from two possible roots. In Latin the verb *nitere* means to shine and so nitency is a bright, lustrous quality. The second meaning takes the Latin verb *niti*, which means to strive, and so nitency means to put in effort and endeavour.

He set about the task with a nitency bordering on the manic.

~

Noctambulation: Noctambulation can refer either to the act of sleepwalking or to taking a pleasurable stroll at night.

I tend to take the dog out for a noctambulation late at night.

~

Nocuous: A rare word far less used than its antonym innocuous. Nocuous comes from the Latin *nocēre*, meaning to harm, so anything nocuous is that which is potentially painful or likely to cause distress.

She caused quite a scene at the party with her bitchy and nocuous comments and remarks.

~

Nomenclature: A slightly controversial word as, strictly speaking, nomenclature derives from the Latin word *nomenclatura*, meaning the assigning of names or the process of naming things. Often, however, nomenclature is just used to mean the name of something.

As my Asian students had names that were difficult for me to pronounce, I got them to choose an English nomenclature for them to use in class.

~

Nosism: Nosism is derived from the Latin *nos*, meaning we, and relates to the somewhat pompous use of the royal we when making statements or giving opinions. An extended, related meaning of nosism is a form of conceited snobbery or pride.

Her tendency to nosism was an affectation designed to mask her humble upbringing.

~

Nostrum: A nostrum is a secret, often highly questionable, medicinal remedy. The word is thought to have developed from the word *noster*, which means ours. This has led etymologists to speculate that the word developed through travelling salesmen dispensing remedies advertised as unique, homemade concoctions.

The manifesto proved to be a nostrum, ill thought out for tackling key issues in the country.

~

Noumenon versus Phenomenon versus Phenomenal: Noumenon and phenomenon are opposites and the difference in meaning is related to perception. In the philosophy of Immanuel Kant (1724–1804) a distinction is drawn between an object as it is in itself (noumenon) and an object as we perceive and experience it through our senses, thoughts and feelings (phenomenon). The much overused adjective phenomenal derives from this distinction and really should only be used to describe things so miraculous and remarkable that they have to be seen to be believed.

It was a phenomenal achievement, extraordinary in every sense.

~

Nuance: Nuance means subtle differences and distinctions. *Nuer* in French, meaning shade or colour, evolved into nuance. This term was introduced into the English language in the late eighteenth century and can be used to describe variations not only in colour but in music, tastes and so forth.

There was definitely a nuance in his latest rendition of the song.

Obdurate: Derived from the Latin word for hard or to harden – *durus*. Obdurate at one time was used quite negatively (and still is) to describe a person implacable and stubborn in their ideas and opinions. However, a secondary meaning suggests that obdurate can also mean someone who sticks to their principles.

I tried very hard to argue my point but she became more and more obdurate that I was wrong.

≈

Obeah: Obeah is a word of African origin and relates to a particular type of faith-healing or voodoo practised traditionally in parts of the British West Indies.

In the crowd at the cricket match in Kingston was a man dressed as a witch-doctor; he claimed to be a master of Obeah and predicted the result of the game.

≈

Obeisance: In the fourteenth century the Anglo-French verb *obeir* meant to obey. Obeisance has the meaning of showing, through words or action, an acknowledgement of respect for something or someone, as in bowing before a monarch.

'Not the least obeisance made he; not a minute stopped or stayed he;
But, with mien of lord or lady, perched above my chamber door.'

Edgar Allan Poe, *The Raven* (1845)

≈

Obelize: The *obulus* was a mark, very similar to the mathematical division symbol, that was appended to ancient manuscripts to question something of spurious truth or veracity. From this word comes the very rare verb obelize, which means to question if something is authentic or fabricated.

It is so hard not to feel that there should be better systems to obelize some of the nonsense published in newspapers.

∾

Obfuscate: Part of the stem for obfuscate comes from the Latin word for to darken or a dark brown colour, *fuscus*. It roughly translates as to make something muddy or to throw a shadow over it. Either way, it's about making something unclear and difficult to comprehend.

The authorities made various attempts to obfuscate the findings of the official enquiry into the disaster.

∾

Objurgation: Although the Latin word for law is *jur* (think of legal words like jurisprudence), an objurgation is a severe telling off for doing something wrong.

I received a severe objurgation from my mother for my drunken antics at a family wedding.

∾

Obliquity and Obreptitious: Obliquity has several meanings: it can be either a deviation from sound thought or moral rectitude, or it can be deliberately obscuring something through words or actions. Similarly, obreptitious is an adjective describing something achieved by trickery or concealment.

Finnegans Wake, by James Joyce, is full of the most impenetrable obliquities.

∾

Oblivescence: Oblivescence is the act or process of forgetting something, often fleetingly.

I have a real problem with short-term oblivescence; increasingly, I have to write down lists to remember key things.

∾

Obsequious: The word obsequious derives from the Latin *obsequium*, meaning compliance. An obsequious person is basically a shameless, fawning brown nose who curries favour through flattery to further their own ends.

The novels of Charles Dickens contain some of the most grotesquely obsequious characters in English literature.

～

Obvolute: In botany, obvolute refers to plants and flowers that have overlapping leaves or petals (think of a rosebud). The adjective is also used to describe narratives where separate stories overlap.

The film Pulp Fiction *has an obvolute narrative structure, whereby five different stories converge at different points.*

～

Oculate, Oculiform and Oculus: *Oculus* in Latin is the word for eye so anything oculate is eye-like in manner or action. Oculiform is more descriptive and describes abstractions and shapes that may resemble eyes. Finally oculus is the traditional word for a round or oval-shaped window in a building.

The signature design of many art deco buildings included oculus-shaped openings, almost like portholes on huge cruise ships.

～

Odium: The Latin verb *odisse*, meaning to hate, provides the link to odium. To be subjected to odium is to be almost universally despised and loathed, usually because of prior actions and reputation.

The deposed dictator cannot have been unaware of the odium his country felt towards him.

～

Oenology and Oenophile: Oenology is the study and science of wine making, covering all aspects from production to tasting and classification. An oenophile is someone who loves, or is obsessed with, all things wine-related – a connoisseur.

I'm thinking of taking a course in oenology.

~

Oikology: This is a fancy, possibly spurious term for the science of good house-keeping, considered especially in respect of sanitary conditions and cleanliness.

I tried to convince my wife that she was an oikologist but she wasn't having any of it and handed me a mop and bucket.

~

Oleaginous: It seems hard to believe that a word most commonly associated with slimy, slithery, not to be trusted, heralds from the humble olive tree. Oleaginous comes directly from the Latin *oleagineus*, meaning from an olive tree, the fruit of which produces olive oil. As an adjective it describes an oily and slimy disposition or anything oil-like.

The oleaginous behaviour of the journalist during the interview was frankly stomach-churning.

~

Olid: An olid smell is something really nasty and foetid.

The bins outside the restaurant were thoroughly olid and clearly hadn't been cleaned for weeks.

~

Ominate: The verb to ominate is closely linked to the word omen and shares the same feeling of foreboding. To ominate is to make a prophecy or to act as the agent of a prophecy or omen.

The old guy has been ominating the end of the world for years.

~

Omnipotent versus Omniscient: Omnipotent originally referred specifically to the power held by an almighty God. *Omni* means all in Latin and *potens* potent or powerful (hence all-powerful). Gods are also described as omniscient, which means all-knowing and all-seeing. Omnipotent is often used to refer to tyrannical despots and, increasingly, information technology organizations.

The once seemingly omnipotent technology company is increasingly coming under attack for the way it shares clients' personal data.

~

Oneirocritic: In Greek *oneiros* is the word for dreams and *krites* means judge; an oneirocritic, then, is somebody who interprets dreams.

Sigmund Freud was probably the most famous oneirocritic in history, though he probably preferred the term psychoanalyst.

~

Onomasticon: A rather highbrow noun for a collection or listing of words grouped by a common subject (science or medicine etc.) or purpose, such as a glossary of key words.

This book is an onomasticon of unusual or misunderstood words.

~

Operose: Derived from the Latin word *operosus*, meaning full of work, operose has come to mean laborious, time-consuming and even tedious.

Moving house is an operose endeavour that seems to drag on forever.

~

Opprobrium and Opprobrious: In the seventeenth century *probrum* was frankly bad behaviour. The Latin word gave rise to the noun opprobrium, meaning something that has brought disgrace or infamy. The adjective opprobrious relates to harsh and damning criticism.

The major banks faced widespread public opprobrium over the payments of bonuses to chief executives.

~

Opusculum and Opuscula: In English, opus (Latin for work) can refer to any literary or artistic creation, though it often specifically refers to a musical piece. *Culum* is a diminutive suffix and so an opusculum is a small or minor work by an artist, writer or musician. Opuscula is an adjective derived from this.

Debussy's short solo piano pieces are great examples of opuscula art.

~

Oracular: The Oracle of Delphi was, for the Ancient Greeks, the font of all knowledge. A sacred shrine inhabited by the Pythia, in times of strife people would visit the oracle hoping for guidance through troubled times. Oracular describes any oracle-like pronouncement or anything resembling or pertaining to an oracle.

The Pythia delivered their judgements with solemn discretion.

~

Ordure: Ordure is a very polite word for what our body excretes, particularly through the anus. Derived from the Middle French word *ord*, meaning foul or horrid – ordure is also waste or decay and is sometimes used figuratively to describe something going down the pan, so to speak.

The nation's obsession with reality television represents the cultural ordure of modern times.

~

Orgiastic: Orgiastic relates simply to orgies or wild and unabashed celebrations (not necessarily in the sexual sense of an orgy).

The orgiastic scenes at the masquerade ball resembled a painting by Hieronymus Bosch.

~

Orison: An orison, traditionally, is a prayer given to God for help or guidance. In modern terms an orison can also be a plea or impassioned request.

The Pope delivered an emotive orison asking for divine guidance in bringing about a peaceful solution to the grave international crisis.

~

Orotund: The Roman poet Horace is credited with coining the Latin phrase *ore rotundo*, meaning to speak with a rounded mouth. Orotund in English means to speak clearly and with strength of purpose and delivery.

His orotund speech to the conference had the delegates on their feet, enthusiastically applauding.

~

Otiose: A relatively recent word, otiose first appeared in English in the late eighteenth century to describe things that produce little of use or worth. Over time, the word started to be applied to people, particularly people of an idle or slack disposition when it came to matters of work, and developed a rather quaint meaning of being at leisure.

An otiose young man of independent means, he never did a hard day's work in his life.

P
~

Pachydermatous: Pachydermatous, meaning thick skinned, is derived from Greek and was adopted by the French zoologist, Georges Culvier, in the late 1700s to classify thick-skinned, hoofed mammals such as elephants, rhinoceroses and hippopotamuses (*pachydermata*). It can also be used to describe a callous, insensitive person.

A pachydermatous person feels nothing for the rough sleeper in the doorway.

~

Paean: A song, hymn or speech that praises the virtues of someone or something, a paean is written in honour of its subject. In Greek mythology, Paean was physician to the gods and the earliest musical paeans were hymns of praise and thanksgiving to Apollo who, according to Homer, on occasions took the guise of Paean. Originally sung at festivals, funerals or when marching into battle, over time a paean has come to mean some kind of tribute.

There wasn't a dry eye at the funeral when Tom read the paean he had written for his brother.

~

Paladin: A paladin is a leader of a cause or a trusted military leader. Deriving from Palatine Hill, the location of the Roman emperors' palace in Rome, over time the word has picked up various meanings in Latin-based languages, and it has made its way into English to also denote a palace.

During the Second World War, Churchill was a paladin of the British people.

~

Palisade: Deriving from the Latin noun *palus*, meaning stake, a palisade is a line of defensive sharp stakes and also a line of tall cliffs.

The fifteen-mile-long stretch of cliffs along the bank of the Hudson River is named 'the Palisades' and, purportedly, got their name due to their resemblance to tall rows of stakes or trees.

~

Palliate: To palliate is to reduce violence or obvious symptoms without curing the underlying problem (e.g. palliative care). It is also used to describe the covering up of an action with excuses and apologies. The Ancient Romans used the word *pallium* to describe the cloak-like garb that was worn by the Greeks as opposed to their own togas. The word gradually evolved to form palliate, which, rather than referring to a cloak you wear, took on the figurative idea of a cloak of protection. The word is now used to gloss over or whitewash something bad.

The government tried to palliate its lack of progress with the report on poverty by announcing a new public holiday.

~

Panjandrum: A panjandrum is a powerful person or pretentious official. It was concocted by the eighteenth-century British actor, Samuel Foote, and was, apparently, part of a made-up line of gibberish intended to test the memory of a fellow actor who claimed that he could repeat anything after hearing it only once. The word was used seventy-five years later by Maria Edgeworth in a book of children's stories and eventually became part of general vocabulary.

The parking officer acted like a panjandrum when issuing me the ticket.

~

Paradigm: A paradigm is a very clear or typical example of something. The word derives from the Latin *paradigm* and the Greek *paradeiknynai*, meaning to show side by side.

Her latest bestseller is a paradigm of what a good detective novel should be.

~

Peccable: Used to describe someone of weak character who is susceptible to temptation and likely or prone to sin. Peccable derives from *peccare*, the Latin for sin.

The judge described the defendant as a peccable individual.

~

Pedantry: Pedantry is practised by pedants and describes an excessive attention to detail, especially in relation to knowledge. The word pedant is generally used in a pejorative sense in English; however, the word derives from the French *pédant* and Italian *pedante*, both of which mean teacher or schoolmaster.

His pedantry, especially concerning the misuse of words, can often become tiresome in social situations.

~

Peignoir: A peignoir is a woman's loose nightgown or negligée and first came into use in the mid-nineteenth century. It is derived from the French word *pengner*, to comb the hair, which itself is based on the Latin *pectin*, comb.

Wearing a blue peignoir, she sat at the mirror combing her golden hair.

~

Pejorative: Used to describe belittling or disparaging remarks, a pejorative comment has negative connotations and derives from the Latin *pejorare*, meaning to make things worse or aggravate. The term only seems to have been in use in the English language since the late 1880s.

He strongly objected to being referred to as a Philistine as he found it highly pejorative.

~

Pelf: Pelf derives from the Anglo-French word *pelfre*, meaning stolen goods, the ancestor of the English verb to pilfer. By the beginning of the sixteenth century people began to use pelf with reference generally to money or riches.

The landlord seemed to care more about pelf than about the living conditions of his tenants.

~

Pensive: The Anglo-French word *penser*, meaning to think, derives from the Latin *pensare*, meaning to ponder. In English, pensive is often used to describe moods, particularly people who are apprehensive and anxious. The original meaning of the word is simply to think deeply, often about something sad or regrettable.

The wet winter days often put her in a pensive state of mind.

~

Penumbra: Although literally meaning a partial illumination, as in an eclipse, penumbra is also used to refer to something that covers, surrounds or obscures, e.g. a shroud, and also to a 'grey area' where things are not just black or white. Deriving from the Latin words *paene*, meaning almost, and *umbra*, which is shadow, penumbra is often used as a legal term to refer to an area within which distinction or resolution is difficult or uncertain.

The defendant was advised that the verdict could go either way as this was a penumbra.

~

Perdition: Originating from the Latin *perdere*, to destroy, the first known use of the word perdition was in the fourteenth century. It means utter destruction or eternal damnation.

All sinners are condemned to perdition.

~

Peremptory: Peremptory, meaning giving no opportunity for debate, derives from the Latin *perimere*, meaning to take entirely or destroy. It is commonly used to describe a dictatorial manner, intolerance, and disregard for the opinion of others.

I felt that my employer gave me no opportunity to make my point due to his peremptory manner.

~

Perfidy: Meaning disloyalty or an act of treachery, perfidy derives from the Latin *perfidus*, meaning faithless.

He found it very hard to come to terms with his wife's perfidy.

~

Perfunctory: Perfunctory describes something that is done with little care or effort or by someone lacking enthusiasm. First appearing in English in the late sixteenth century, it derives from the Latin *perfunctorius*, meaning done in a careless or superficial manner.

When he was asked by his mother to tidy his bedroom, he did it in a perfunctory manner.

~

Periphery: From the Greek *periphereia*, and first used in English around 1568, the periphery is an external boundary of something, an area lying beyond the designated limits of a thing.

Despite the apparent affluence of the city, some of the poorest housing conditions exist on the periphery.

~

Permeable, Pervious and Impervious: Permeable and pervious are synonyms and relate in science to the ability of an element to pass through an object or substance (such as light or liquids). The adjective impervious has a wider meaning related to a character and behaviour. A person impervious to criticism, for example, doesn't let it affect them (or maybe they just don't listen) so it doesn't pass through into them. Similarly, the air can be permeated with the smell of freshly baking bread (because the smell is passing through the air).

He seemed impervious to the criticisms levelled at him.

~

Peroration: Peroration is the concluding section of a speech and can also refer to a long and rhetorical oration. It derives from the Latin *orare*, meaning to speak or plead.

After an hour of listening to the sermon, we were grateful when the vicar reached the peroration.

~

Persiflage: Meaning frivolous banter, persiflage was adopted from French in the eighteenth century. The word originated from the French verb *persifler*, meaning to banter and formed from the prefix *per*, meaning thoroughly, and *sifler*, which is to whistle, hiss or boo.

His persiflage, although said tongue in cheek, sometimes offends those who don't really know him.

~

Phlegmatic: This word derives from phlegm, one of the four bodily fluids called humours by the Ancient Greeks and believed by them to control human personalities, each humour being associated with one of the four basic elements: air, fire, earth and water. Phlegm was linked to water, the cold element; hence describing a person's character as being phlegmatic denotes a cool, calm and unemotional personality.

She always stayed phlegmatic whatever the situation.

~

Pidgin: Pidgin is a simplified form of speech created to enable people of different languages to communicate and was first devised in the early nineteenth century by English and Chinese merchants to facilitate trading. Over time the word 'business' had modified into 'Pidgin' and it began to be used to describe the unique communication used by people who speak different languages. Pidgins normally contain small vocabularies but a few have grown to become used as a native language, e.g. Sea Island Creole, Haitian Creole and Louisiana Creole.

Over time they seemed to understand each other by adopting a form of pidgin English.

~

Piebald: Commonly associated with horses, piebald denotes something made up of incompatible parts, or colours, especially spotted or blotched with black and white, and its first recorded use was in 1590. Rooted in the Latin *pica* (*Pica pica* being the scientific name for a magpie), the word is made up of the word pie (another name for magpie) and bald, which, apart from a lack of hair, can also mean marked with white.

I put my money on the piebald horse, which, although odd in colour, was actually rather attractive.

~

Piliferous: Piliferous means to bear or produce hairs.

She noticed that her teenage son was beginning to display a piliferous chin.

~

Plebiscite: Deriving from the Latin *plebis scitum*, which was a law voted by decree of the common people, plebiscite means a vote by the inhabitants of an entire country or district in which they can opt for or against a proposal or on a choice of government or leader.

There is to be a plebiscite to elect a new mayor.

❧

Plenipotentiary: First coming into use during the mid-seventeenth century, plenipotentiary means a person invested with full authority to transact business. It derives from the Latin root *plenus*, meaning full, and *potens*, being powerful. The term can be used, for example, to describe someone sent as an ambassador to another country with full power to act on behalf of his or her government.

The newly appointed ambassador to Washington attended the banquet with other plenipotentiaries.

❧

Pleonasm: Stemming from the Greek verb *pleonazein*, meaning to be excessive, pleonasm is another word for redundancy. Pleonasms are additional words that are used to add emphasis or to get a message across to an audience, but that are not technically necessary.

There is no such thing as an 'extra bonus' or a 'free gift'; those are merely pleonasms.

❧

Plethora: Coming from the Greek, meaning fullness, plethora was first used in the sixteenth century when describing certain medical conditions that caused redness and swelling due to an excess volume of blood. In modern times the word has come to mean profusion, excess or abundance.

In the springtime the garden is decked with a plethora of colours.

❧

Plunder: In use since the mid-seventeenth century, plunder describes the taking of something, e.g. the taking of land during war, or to take something by robbery or swindling.

When the archaeologists opened the tomb they were disappointed to find that it had already been plundered.

~

Pluvial: Pluvial relates to rain and is derived from the Latin word *pluvia*. During the seventeenth century clerics wore long cloaks known as pluvials as protection from the rain when taking part in processions, and in the nineteenth century the word was adopted as a term describing a period of higher-than-average rainfall or with reference to things produced by rain, such as pluvial lakes or pluvial erosion.

The pluvial weather this summer has caused many outdoor events to be cancelled.

~

Polemic: A strong verbal or written argument against another's ideas or beliefs, polemic was first introduced into the English language (borrowed from the French *polemique*) during the seventeenth century. It is derived from the Greek word *polemikos*, meaning warlike or hostile.

Her article was a polemic against the apparent rise of the far right in European politics.

~

Pooh-bah: Pooh-Bah is a character in Gilbert and Sullivan's opera *The Mikado* (1885) bearing the title Lord-High-Everything-Else. A somewhat pompous and self-important man, the term pooh-bah has come to mean anyone who holds lots of grandiose titles and positions.

Since retiring from mainstream politics the former minister has fashioned himself into a pooh-bah by accepting many directorships and high-level positions.

~

Popinjay: Originally this was the English name for a parrot, deriving from the French *perroquet*. To be called a popinjay would have been thought of as a compliment prior to the mid-1500s, when parrots were rare and exotic. However, once parrots became more commonplace in England, the term started to be used in a derogatory fashion to describe a person who was vulgar and gaudy.

He arrived at the dinner dressed like a popinjay and looked completely out of place.

~

Precatory: Precatory means to express a wish and derives from the Latin *precari*, which means to pray. In the legal sense it is used to request that something be done, but the request is not legally binding. It can also be used to request, for example, that a certain dress code is adhered to at an occasion or event but, again, this is not legally binding.

My aunt made a precatory request in her will that, after her death, I look after Tiddles. However, I am allergic to cats and undecided what to do.

~

Predicate: To predicate is to found or base an argument or assertion upon a particular idea or instance. The word can also be used in formal grammar to define the part of a sentence or clause that expresses a description of the subject.

His whole argument was predicated on the fallacy that people trust politicians.

~

Presage: The meaning of the noun presage is an omen, an intuition of what is going to happen in the future. The verb presage is to prophesy and both meanings derive from the Latin prefix *prae*, meaning before or prior to, alongside the adjective *sagus*, meaning prophetic. Unlike predict or prediction, which implies that some form of logic is used in coming to a conclusion, presage is based on a feeling of what is going to happen.

She knew nothing about the odds of winning but had a strong presage her numbers would come up on the lottery that week.

~

Prestidigitation: Meaning sleight of hand, prestidigitation is composed of the French word *preste*, derived from the Italian *presto*, meaning quick or nimble, and the Latin word *digitus*, which is a finger.

We were really impressed with the prestidigitation of the magician we saw last night. Despite sitting in the front row at the theatre, we could not work out how the trick was done.

～

Primogeniture: The firstborn child of the same parents is in the position of being primogeniture. Primogeniture played a key role in English inheritance law, meaning that the eldest male offspring was entitled to inherit all property of the family estate. The word is derived from the Latin *primus*, meaning first, and *genitura*, being birth.

Due to primogeniture, Mary's older twin brother (by fifteen minutes) was entitled to inherit the family home.

～

Progeny: A progeny is a descent or offspring. Deriving from the Latin verb *progignere*, meaning to beget, the word first came into the English language during the fourteenth century.

A large percentage of Americans are the progeny of Irish immigrants.

～

Prolixity: Derived from the Latin term *prolixus*, meaning extended or copious, prolixity describes overly wordy, verbose speech or writing. Rather than getting to the point of what needs to be said, prolixity in discourse flows needlessly on and on.

The father of the bride made a speech of such prolixity that by the time it finally ended we were almost falling asleep.

～

Promethean: In Greek mythology Prometheus fashioned humans from clay and taught them art and culture. In order for civilization to progress, Prometheus stole fire from the underworld and bequeathed it to the human race. This so enraged Zeus that, as punishment, Prometheus was chained to a rock to be pecked at by a giant eagle for all eternity. Any artistic endeavour that is original and ground-breaking is often described as promethean. A rarer sense is to use promethean to describe any long period of intense suffering, as that endured by Prometheus himself.

Banksy was at the forefront of the promethean graffiti art movement.

∽

Promulgate: Meaning to proclaim, promulgate is usually associated with some form of public declaration. Its origin is the Latin *promulgates: pro*, meaning forward and *mulgare*, meaning to extract.

On election night it was promulgated that the government managed to stay in power with a slim majority.

∽

Propinquity: Propinquity and the more commonly used word proximity are very similar in meaning (both deriving from the Latin root *prope*, meaning near) and are interchangeable, each meaning nearness. However, propinquity, the older of the two words by a hundred years, though both entered the English language in the fourteenth century, implies a stronger sense of closeness.

They chose to buy their current home due to the propinquity of an excellent high school.

∽

Propitiate: To propitiate is to endeavour to gain or regain goodwill. This word is most commonly used to refer to an attempt to avert the anger of a superior being or god.

The natives made sacrifices to the god of the mountain in the belief that this would propitiate his anger and prevent the volcano erupting.

∽

Pseudologist: Deriving from the word *pseudologe*, meaning to speak falsely, a pseudologist is someone who tells lies.

After closely watching his body language, I have come to the conclusion that he is a pseudologist.

∽

Puerile: Although now used to describe, in a negative manner, the childish or immature behaviour of an adult, puerile was originally the term used to refer specifically to the behaviour of a child. Puerile derives from the Latin noun *puer*, meaning boy or child.

His puerile behaviour was frowned upon by many of his colleagues in the office.

∽

Pugnacious: Derived from the Latin *pugnare*, to fight, and introduced into English in the seventeenth century, pugnacious is used to describe someone who has an argumentative and confrontational manner.

She always felt apprehensive before she was due to meet with her pugnacious boss.

∽

Puissant: To be puissant is to be powerful. The word derives from the Latin *posse*, meaning to be able, as do the words power and potent.

She gave a puissant speech about human rights.

∽

Pulchritude: Pulchritude means physical beauty and has been in use in the English language since the fifteenth century. It is descended from the Latin word *pulcher*, meaning beautiful and attractive.

Her pulchritude was the envy of all the women in the village.

∽

Punctilio: Punctilio comes from the Italian word *puntiglio*, meaning point of honour or scruple, and refers to observance of a detailed code of conduct or a careful observance of appropriate social conduct.

It is a requirement that all carefully observe the punctilio during the coronation ceremony.

∾

Purloin: Deriving from the Anglo-French word *purluigner*, meaning to set aside, purloin means to misappropriate or steal, often by breach of trust.

The security guards were employed to check the bags of all staff to ensure there was no purloining of company stock.

∾

Putsch: A putsch is another name for a *coup d'état*, a secret and swift attempt to overthrow a government. The Swiss German word *putsch* originally meant knock or thrust and began to be used to refer to numerous attempts to overthrow the government in Weimar Germany.

The recent coup in Zimbabwe fortunately turned out to be a bloodless putsch.

Q

∾

Quantal: There are two uses for the word quantal: the first describes the outcome of scientific experiments where only one of two possible outcomes can result and derives from the Latin *quantum*, meaning how much? The second refers to the smallest possible unit of a form of energy.

In this experiment the gas will turn green or yellow depending on how many quantal units of energy are absorbed.

∾

Quiddity and Quirk: Quiddity dates back to the fourteenth century and means the essence or substance of something; it typifies what a thing is. From quiddity came quibble, meaning a trivial or small point, which arose to describe the trickier points argued over by sixteenth-century academics. Like quiddity, quirk also derives from the Latin pronoun *quis*, meaning who, and, also like quiddity, it can refer to a person's unique eccentricities.

The portrait painter managed to capture the quiddity of his subject.

~

Quidnunc: Quidnunc, meaning busybody, literally translates from the Latin for what now? The earliest reference to a gossiper as a quidnunc appeared in *The Tatler* in 1709.

Keep your voice down, the local quidnunc is trying to eavesdrop on our conversation.

~

Quietus: The noun quietus was introduced into the English language in the 1500s to mean the discharge or exemption of an outstanding debt, coming from medieval Latin, *quietus est*, meaning he is quit. Later, Shakespeare used the word quietus in *Hamlet* to mean the end of life. A later nineteenth-century adaptation uses quietus in the phrase 'put the quietus on', meaning something that quietens or represses.

Having been lucky enough to win the lottery, Susan decided that she would grant a quietus on the money her friend owed her.

~

Quincunx: An arrangement of five objects in a square or rectangle with one at each corner and one in the middle. Originally the name for an Ancient Roman coin with a weight equal to five-twelfths of a *libra*, a quincunx was symbolized by a pattern of five dots, the name deriving from the Latin roots *quinque*, meaning five, and *uncia*, meaning one-twelfth. In the sixteenth century the term was adopted into the English language to mean patterns using the distinctive five-dot arrangement.

The gardener planted the flowers to form a quincunx.

~

Quintessence: In medieval Latin *quinta essentia* meant the fifth essence. At the time, people still thought that the earth was made up of four elements – earth, air, fire and water – and that the stars and planets contained a fifth element, believing that if they could isolate this fifth essence they would be able to use it to cure all disease. Despite this theory finally being discounted, the word quintessence remains in the English language as meaning the purest essence of something.

There is no doubt that Adolf Hitler was the quintessence of evil.

~

Quisling: The word quisling, meaning a traitor or collaborator, was first used in the English language during 1940 and was a direct reference to Vidkun Quisling, a Norwegian army officer and fascist who sold out his country to Adolf Hitler. In return for his cooperation, the Nazis set Quisling up as the figurehead of the puppet government during Norway's occupation.

Most quislings were sentenced to death at the Nuremberg War Trials.

~

Quixotic: Quixotic derives directly from Miguel de Cervantes' (1547–1616) celebrated Renaissance novel *Don Quixote*. The hero of the novel is a foolish romantic, driven by rash but unattainable ideals. In English, quixotic is often used to describe plans or ideas that are unrealistic or overly imaginative and optimistic.

His head is full of quixotic plans and ideas, none of which ever come to fruition.

~

Quondam: Quondam was introduced into the English language in the sixteenth century, deriving from the Latin *quondam*, meaning at one time or formerly. Other more unusual ways of saying formerly are whilom, preterit or erstwhile.

He recently took over as head teacher, having been the quondam head of a nearby school.

R

~

Rabelaisian: François Rabelais (1494–1553) was a French monk, writer and scholar, and he is responsible for introducing the word gargantuan (enormous) into the English language. The word Rabelaisian usually refers to writing or speech that is bawdy or coarse in nature or subject, although this definition seems a little harsh on Rabelais, who was a talented scholar and polymath and whose writings are considered masterpieces of medieval European literature.

The best man's speech took on a distinctly Rabelaisian flavour when describing the groom's antics while playing for the university rugby team.

~

Rachitis and Rachitic: Rachitis is an old-fashioned word for rickets – a medical disorder that affects children due to a deficiency of vitamin D and calcium. Rachitic is an adjectival form to describe deformities caused by this debilitating condition.

Alexander Pope suffered from poor health throughout his life, especially in childhood, leaving him hunchbacked due to a rachitic spine.

~

Rambunctious: A colourful word that entered into North American English in the mid-nineteenth century. The origins of rambunctious are unclear but it is thought to be a distortion of an older British English adjective rumbumptious, meaning marked by boisterousness and exuberance.

The crowd at the game were loud and rambunctious, singing and chanting throughout the match.

~

Ramification: Ramification is a word with various meanings that have evolved organically over time. Derived from the Middle French verb (via Latin) *ramificare*, meaning to spread out into different parts, ramification is the act of growing outwards like the branches of a tree or stems of a plant. A modern definition, more commonly used, is that which describes unforeseen and often negative consequences of an action or situation.

The government's fiscal policies could have serious ramifications for the whole country.

~

Rancour: Derived from an Old French word describing bitterness and resentment which developed from the Latin word *rancorem*, meaning a rancid and horrible smell, rancour is used predominantly in the context of arguments or disputes between two individuals or groups.

The historical rancour between the two countries is so deep set that any settlement over the border issue will be fraught with difficulties.

~

Rankle: Rankle means to cause anger, irritation or bitterness, but when it was first introduced into the English language at the beginning of the seventeenth century it meant to fester and was linked to the French noun *raoncle* or *draoncle*, which was a festering sore.

The manager appeared rankled by the chants of the opposition's fans.

~

Rapacious: The practice of rapine is historically associated with outlaws such as pirates, and means stealing through force and violence. Rapacious derives from the Latin word *rapere*, meaning to seize, but is often related to the desires or needs that drive actions. Someone with a rapacious appetite is essentially just plain greedy.

He had a rapacious appetite for fried food.

~

Rapprochement: The first known usage of the word rapprochement in English dates from 1809 at the height of the Napoleonic Wars. It is perhaps fitting then that the word derives from the French word *rapprocher*, meaning to approach or establish closeness. Rapprochement is used mostly in the context of building bridges between two conflicting groups and establishing (or re-establishing) peaceful relations.

The rapprochement was in the interests of both sides as the cost of the war was becoming unsustainable.

≈

Rapture: Derived from the Latin *raptus*, the first known use of the word rapture was in 1594. It is an expression or manifestation of ecstasy or passion; an intense exaltation of mind and feelings; an experience of being carried away by overwhelming emotion. According to Christian theology, the Rapture is the final assumption of Christians into heaven.

He was almost driven to rapture by the exquisite beauty of the sight which he beheld.

≈

Rareripe: This is a botanical term for a fruit or vegetable that ripens early in a season, such as rareripe plums. Rareripe can also be used as an adjective to describe someone who reaches their potential at an early age.

The actor had a rareripe talent at an early age but his later films let him down.

≈

Ratiocination: Ratiocination is the name for a logical train of thought and dates from the late Renaissance period during which there were radical advances in the arts and sciences. The word is an extension of the Latin word *ratio*, meaning reason or method.

Francis Bacon's grounding in classical learning provided him with considerable skills of ratiocination.

~

Recalcitrant: From the Latin word *recalcitrāre*, meaning to kick backwards or kick with the heels, recalcitrant is commonly used to describe a person who is stubborn or obstinate, especially with regard to authority. A secondary usage is often applied to objects, particularly machines, which are malfunctioning.

He'd struggled all afternoon with a recalcitrant lawn mower.

~

Recherché: *Rechercher* is a French verb meaning to seek out or search. Marcel Proust's famous novel *À la recherche du temps perdu* translates into English as *In Search of Lost Time* and it is this sense of seeking something rare or exotic that provides the meaning for recherché. The word also has an air of refinement about it. Recherché tastes in some particular aspect such as food and wine evoke expertise and exquisite choice.

He had recherché tastes in jazz music.

~

Recidivism: Recidivism derives from the Latin verb *recidere*, meaning to fall back, and describes a tendency to relapse into a previous condition or mode of behaviour. Recidivism is often used in the context of the criminal justice system, when offenders relapse into criminal behaviour on release from penal institutions.

Recidivism is a major problem in the penal system.

~

Reconnoitre: Derived from Old French, to reconnoitre is the act of inspecting or surveying an area of land. Originally a military term (as in providing a reconnaissance of the enemy's position), the word can also be used as a slightly pompous description of taking a casual stroll around an unfamiliar environment.

After a hearty lunch in the hotel restaurant, our group went out into the streets to reconnoitre the surrounding area.

~

Recreant: The Anglo-French word *recreire*, meaning to give up, provides the root for recreant. As a noun, a recreant is somebody who deserts their duty through cowardice or self-interest. As an adjective, it describes cowardly actions and behaviour.

The recreant pleas of the prisoners for mercy fell on deaf ears.

∼

Recrudescence: Closely related to reoccurrence and, in medical terms, relapse, recrudescence is a curious word that often relates to medical conditions. Although elegant sounding, it has generally negative connotations. A recrudescence is a renewal of a volatile situation or state after a period of stability or calm.

I thought my shingles outbreak had subsided but I experienced a recrudescence of the virus.

∼

Rectitude: Pertaining mainly to matters of morality and ethics, rectitude appeared in Old French and late Middle English from the fourteenth century onwards. The word describes straightness and clarity of purpose in decision making or personal beliefs.

Jake's rectitude prevented him from lying to the police about his actions.

∼

Recumbent: Somebody in a recumbent position is lying down or reclining. The noun refers to those terrifying bicycles whereby the rider lies on their back with the pedals above them.

He sat in a recumbent position with his legs injudiciously spread.

∼

Recurrent: Recurrent used to mean turning back or moving in the opposite direction, as it derives from the Latin *recurrere*, meaning running back. This lack of progress in one direction led to recurrent being used to mean something that occurs over and over again, like recurrent back pain or recurrent (often anti-social) behaviour patterns or problems.

He had several weeks off work with a recurrent illness.

~

Recusant: Originally, a recusant was a Catholic dissenter in sixteenth-, seventeenth- and eighteenth-century Britain. The word has come to mean anyone who wilfully rejects authority or official regulations. In legal terminology, a recusant is a person who fails to attend court, either to answer a charge or as a summoned witness.

He had become a recusant when it came to paying the poll tax.

~

Redivivus: An adjective that describes a state of renewal or rebirth. *Vivus* is the Latin word for living, so with the addition of the prefix *re* (in Latin, meaning return) the word becomes reliving.

Hebrew is a successful example of a redivivus language.

~

Redolent: A melancholy word often used to describe nostalgic memories. Redolent, in the strictest sense, relates to smells and fragrances. The human sense of smell evokes memories, and redolent is often used to describe scents that bring forth recollections.

The smell of freshly baked bread was always redolent of his grandmother's kitchen.

~

Redoubtable: Closely related to the French word *redouter*, which means to dread something, the meaning of redoubtable has changed. Originally, the word meant to fear something on the grounds of their power or prowess – for example, the redoubtable Spartan army. Redoubtable has since come to be attached, in an individual sense, to people who are admired or esteemed.

Churchill was a redoubtable speaker in parliamentary debates.

~

Regnant: Regnant principally refers to a ruler or reigning monarch, president or despot. The word usually follows the noun it is modifying and means ruler of a country and its people. A secondary meaning of regnant is to describe prevailing or widespread ideas held by a majority.

Elizabeth I ascended the throne as Queen regnant in 1558.

The political campaign exploited the regnant belief that immigration was out of control.

~

Regrate: A polite word for an often dubious practice. Regrate relates to commerce and, specifically, the buying of commodities at one price with the intention of reselling at another (presumably) higher price in order to make a tidy profit. The word first appears in Old French and late Middle English as early as the fifteenth century, which goes to show that people had been ripping others off long before the creation of the stock markets.

The scandalously low price when the market opened prompted many investors to regrate on the stocks and shares.

~

Rejoinder: Derived from the Middle French word *rejoindre*, meaning a reply or a response, a rejoinder is usually used in the context of arguments and debates or to describe sharp and witty ripostes. The word is also prevalent in legal language and refers to the response of a defendant to the case brought before the court by a plaintiff or claimant.

'I wish I'd said that,' sighed Wilde.

'You will, Oscar, you will,' said Whistler by way of rejoinder.

~

Remunerate: The Latin verb *remunerare* means to recompense or compensate. In modern parlance, however, to remunerate is to pay an equivalent value (usually in money) for a service or personal expenses.

He was handsomely remunerated for his diligence and hard work.

~

Renascent: Something that is renascent has been revived or imbued with renewed vitality and vigour. The word is similar to the word renaissance, meaning rebirth.

After several years in the wilderness, the singer/songwriter genre suddenly had a renascent period.

~

Renitent: A rare alternative to recalcitrant (see above), renitent describes persistent and stubborn opposition, often in the face of extreme pressure.

The rail unions were renitent in rejecting the solution offered by the management during the strike negotiations.

~

Repine: A graceful word first recorded in English in the sixteenth century yet seldom used in contemporary English. To repine is become fretful and discontented, basically to have a good old moan about something or someone.

'Now, however – but I should be a fool, indeed, to repine at my good fortune.'

Charles Dickens, *The Life and Adventures of Nicholas Nickleby* (1838)

~

Resile versus Resilient: The Latin verb *resilire* means to withdraw or recoil and provides the root for both resile and resilient. However, whereas the verb resile means to step away from or renege on a previous position or agreement, resilient is used to describe endurance and the ability to recover from a setback.

The president has stated his attention to resile US support for climate change accords.

~

Retinue: The Anglo-French verb *retenir* means to retain. In the Middle Ages a retainer was a high-ranking servant of nobility and royalty. The word retinue in modern usage describes a collection of people surrounding an important person, such as a politician's team of advisers, press officers and speech writers.

The actress turned up on set with her usual retinue of personal assistants, stylists, lifestyle gurus and personal trainers.

∽

Retrograde: Something described as retrograde is moving in a direction opposite to its natural flow. The term is used scientifically to describe the apparent backwards orbit of certain celestial bodies. In a figurative sense though, retrograde is anything that is regressing in a negative manner.

The current social policies of the government have been criticized as being retrograde and likely to increase poverty.

∽

Reveille: Derived from the French word *reveiller*, meaning to awaken, a reveille is a sound or signal to get up in the mornings. In military terms, the reveille is a bugle blast at sunrise.

The 6 a.m. reveille always came as a shock, wrenching him unceremoniously from the comfort of sleep.

∽

Reverie: Another nostalgic word, a reverie is the state of abstracted thought, a daydream escape from the humdrum realities of life. The word is best illustrated by the composer Claude Debussy in piano compositions such as *Clair de lune* (1905) and *Rêverie* (1890), which evoke a dreamy, sleep-like sensation. Since Debussy, the word reverie has become the name for short wistful piano pieces.

Oh to be lost in a reverie of times past.

∽

Rhapsodic: An adjective derived from the noun rhapsody which describes an effusive and ecstatic tribute to something or someone. Rhapsodies in music are free-form compositions, often of separate movements that suggest improvisation, such as Gershwin's famous swirling jazz-inspired *Rhapsody in Blue* (1924).

He became rhapsodic when describing the wonderful views across the valley from his hotel window.

~

Ribald: As an adjective, ribald means coarseness and vulgarity in speech, as in a ribald riposte, which could be laced with profanities and insults. As a noun, a ribald is a person prone to making crude and offensive comments.

She was shocked when her complaint to the management provoked a ribald two-word response.

~

Rigorist: Rigorism was a stringent and severe form of Catholicism, and the word rigorist is now applied to anybody who is particularly strict and often inflexible on matters of conduct or judgement. Usually a stickler for rules and regulations, a rigorist is a polite word for a jobsworth.

The head of finance was a rigorist when it came to filing claim forms to deadline.

~

Risible: Derived from the Latin verb *ridēre*, meaning to laugh, risible is something that provokes laughter. The word is often used in negative contexts as a synonym for laughable – something so weak, pathetic or inept it is worthy of ridicule. Strictly speaking, however, risible simply means laughter-inducing, negative or otherwise.

Due mostly to the large quantity of alcohol available, his behaviour became increasingly risible as the night wore on.

~

Rixation: A rixation is a rare word for a brawl or a quarrel between individuals or groups.

The thorny issue of the broken garden fence caused a rixation between the neighbours.

~

Rodomontade: A word that has migrated across several languages, from Italian into French and then on into English. Rodomonte was the vain and boastful king in two fifteenth-century epic poems by Italian writers Boiardo and Ariosto. The popularity of the poems gave rise to the French word *rodomontade*, which in turn became rodomont, an English noun meaning a boast or brag. The word rodomont is no longer used in English but the French *rodomontade* can be used as either an adjective or a noun to describe blustering speech or vainglorious character.

The speech was little more than rodomontade designed to deflect attention from the key issues.

~

Rubescent: Rubescent is the state of becoming red in colour or exuding a red glow (as in blushing). The word is a direct borrow from Latin and is linked to the colour of ruby gemstones.

The pollution in the air and the low autumn sun turned the sky rubescent at dusk.

~

Rudimental: Derived from the Latin *rudi* (raw or rude), rudimental was initially used in English in the first half of the sixteenth century to describe a basic principle or element or a basic skill.

Although she didn't claim to be fluent in French, she did have a rudimental knowledge of the language and could manage to make herself understood.

~

Rueful: Dating from the thirteenth century, rueful describes showing or feeling regret for something done or instilling pity or sympathy.

At the end of the interview she knew that she had done badly and gave a rueful smile to the interview panel as she left the room.

~

Ruminate and Rumination: The verb to ruminate has both a literal and figurative meaning. We ruminate over a problem or predicament and weigh up the implications. Animals (especially cattle) ruminate literally by chewing food repeatedly over and over to make it easier to digest. This has given rise to the idiomatic expression 'to chew the cud' or return to a problem again and again in the hope of finding a solution. To think deeply about something should be considered a positive attribute. However, developments in psychology have identified mental rumination as a key symptom of anxiety and depression.

I shall ruminate over the findings of the report before making my decision.

~

Runagate: An archaic word derived from Middle English via Latin, runagate is a distortion of the Spanish Latin-derived word renegade. A runagate was traditionally the name for a deserter from a particular group or cause, but the word also has the connotations of an outcast, vagabond or wanderer.

One of Harry Dean Stanton's most memorable roles was the part of the runagate preacher in the film Wise Blood.

~

Rusticate: A verb describing a very modern lifestyle choice, to rusticate is principally to move to the country to enjoy a more leisurely pace of life. The word rusticated also has a specialized usage in academia (most notably Oxford and Cambridge universities) where it is the process by which a student is expelled from college for a misdemeanour.

Byron's antics at Cambridge are legendary. A constant thorn in the side of the college authorities, he was fortunate not to get rusticated.

S

Sagacious: Sagacious initially had the meaning of having keen senses of perception, particularly a sense of smell but also of sight and sound. However, the modern meaning is of somebody of clever judgement, discerning in the choices that they make.

He was a sagacious judge of character and chose his companions carefully.

Sain: To sain is to cross oneself for good luck or protection. A secondary meaning is to give a blessing (by making the sign of the cross) to another.

A very religious man, the centre-forward is prone to kneel and sain in the moments before a match kicks off.

Salacious: The Latin verb *salire* means to move. From this the word salacious developed as something that excites or provokes physical activity. Given the Freudian view of the necessity of sexual appetites in determining human behaviour, it wasn't long before salacious came to mean that which is rousing or appealing to sexual desire or imagination.

He was accused of making salacious comments to colleagues at the Christmas party.

Saltatory: The archaic meaning, now virtually obsolete, is of anything relating to dancing, as in saltatory movements. In medicine this sense of moving or jumping is replicated in the study of diseases that suddenly leap or jump in severity rather than following a gradual pattern of symptoms.

He watched her walk across the room, swaying with an almost saltatory elegance.

~

Salubrious: A direct borrowing from the Latin word *salubris*, meaning healthy and wholesome. Anything described as salubrious is in good health or good for you.

It became fashionable in the eighteenth century for the upper classes to go to the coast to benefit from the salubrious effects of the sea, water and air.

~

Sanative: From the Latin verb *sanare*, meaning to cure. A sanative is anything that can help to cure illness (medicine) or generally promote good health.

The sanative effects of regular sleep and exercise are well documented.

~

Sanctimonious: For a long time, sanctimonious referred to people possessing sanctity, holiness and pious devotion. Perhaps at one point people got a bit fed up with being compared to the sanctimonious and rebelled. Since the seventeenth century sanctimonious has come to describe people excessively ostentatious in their beliefs and displaying a 'holier than thou' attitude.

The sanctimonious attitude of the king was at odds with his general behaviour.

~

Sanguine, Sangfroid and Sanguinolent: The Latin word for blood is *sanguis*. This word provides the root for three different words with subtle differences in meaning. Sanguine is, in modern usage, used to describe an optimistic and breezy outlook, the idea being that cheerful and positive people must have cheerful and positive blood. Sangfroid (often confused with sanguine) is the capacity to be sturdy and stoic in the face of adversity and put on a dignified and brave face – to be strong-blooded. Sanguinolent relates to traces of blood found in a bodily excretion and is a medical term.

I thought he'd be very upset about losing the competition but he displayed real sangfroid in thanking his opponent.

~

Sapience: Sapience is wisdom and sharpness of judgement learned through time and experience.

He'd gained a natural sapience from his years working as a teacher.

~

Saponaceous: Saponaceous is a new Latin borrowing by scientists that is based on *sapo*, the Latin word for soap. It describes natural substances, like aloe gel or some plant roots, used in making soap or having the properties of soap. The notion that saponaceous could be applied to designate somebody slippery like soap came from Benjamin Disraeli's famous description of Samuel Wilberforce, given in the example below. Wilberforce became known in the press thereafter as 'Soapy Sam'.

Disraeli memorably described Samuel Wilberforce, the Bishop of Oxford, as 'unctuous, oleaginous, saponaceous'.

~

Saporific: Saporific is all about flavour and the sensation of taste; that which excites the taste buds.

The meal was fantastic with a perfect balance of saporific spices tingling and exciting the palate.

~

Sartorial: Sartorial relates to clothes or a tailor and comes from the Latin *sartor*, one who patches or mends. It has been used in English since the mid-nineteenth century.

Despite being a successful businessman he demonstrated poor sartorial taste.

~

Saturnine: The Ancient Romans assigned character traits to people according to their astrological charts and which sign they were born under. Those born under the sign of Saturn were termed saturnine and thought to be dour, cynical and implacable, with an often sardonic attitude towards others.

His saturnine smile wasn't fooling anybody.

∽

Satyagraha: It is an honour to present this noun, which was introduced into English by Mahatma Gandhi (1869–1948). Satyagraha was Gandhi's policy of non-violent civil resistance, which he preached when leader of the Indian Independence Movement. The word derives from a hybrid of Sanskrit terms and translates roughly as 'insistence on truth'. The ideology of Satyagraha provided inspiration for Doctor Martin Luther King's Civil Rights Movement in the United States and other prominent figures who have fought against oppression around the world.

The Truth and Reconciliation Tribunals in South Africa adopted a policy of Satyagraha as a means of reconciling the country with its past.

∽

Satyr: In Greek mythology the satyrs were half-man half-goat woodland dwellers who followed the Greek god Dionysus and had a reputation for indulging in unabashed revelry. In English a satyr is a rather lecherous man infamous for his hedonistic tendencies.

He's like a satyr; once he gets going at a party there is no stopping him.

∽

Savant: Savant derives from the Latin *sapere*, meaning to be wise. In Middle French *savoir* had the meaning to know. The modern meaning in English, however, is much more complex and often relates to someone who exhibits extraordinary brilliance in a particular field of knowledge, typically mathematics or science, but often struggles with the more routine, everyday aspects of general knowledge and understanding. In this sense the somewhat cruel expression idiot-savant emerged, which is often closely, and more politely, linked with the autistic spectrum.

The film Rain Man *details the relationship between two brothers, one a chancer of dubious morality and the other an autistic but highly gifted mathematical savant.*

~

Scaramouch: In the classical Italian theatre of Commedia dell'arte, Scaramouch was a boastful (often Spanish for some reason) and cowardly buffoon. In English in the seventeenth century the word scaramouch became a byword for a gutless and weak rascal. Today it is probably only familiar to people from the lines of the rock song 'Bohemian Rhapsody' by Queen.

Courtly romances were very popular in France in the seventeenth century with their stock characters of the swashbuckling hero, the downtrodden heroine and the scheming scaramouch.

~

Scarify: An awkward verb form that on one level has a medical definition, which is to make cuts or scratches in the skin in order to administer treatments. On another level, to scarify someone is to programmatically scratch away at the surface of their feelings about something; metaphorically, to scratch at a sore subject. Neither definition is anything other than disquieting and unpleasant.

I felt that because he wouldn't let the matter lie, he was deliberately trying to scarify my feelings on a very sensitive issue.

~

Scatological: Oh my, oh my, have I had fun correcting people on the misuse of scatological over the years! The looks on their faces are a picture. Scatological is often erroneously used to describe randomness or lack or order. Total horse dung! No, really, literally, scatological comes from the Greek word *skat*, meaning excrement, which mutated into the Old English word *scearn*, meaning dung. As an adjective, anything scatological, particularly to do with humour, is always toilet or excrement based.

The problem with much modern stand-up comedy is that it relies upon scatological jokes to get cheap laughs.

~

Schadenfreude: Another word often misused and misunderstood. The German word for damage is *schaden* and for joy, *freude*. Hence schadenfreude is taking vicarious pleasure in hearing of other people's misfortune and certainly has nothing at all to do with feeling sorry for oneself.

I couldn't help but feeling a certain shiver of schadenfreude when I heard my ex-girlfriend had split up with her new boyfriend.

~

Schism: Originally, a scientific word to describe a separation in particles or substances. Schism is most commonly used to describe a split inside a group or organization, usually a political party or religious group.

There is a clear schism in the government regarding foreign policy in relation to Europe.

~

Scullion: A lovely word that has remained more or less intact from the Middle English *sculioun* of Chaucer. A scullion is somebody who does lowly jobs in a large kitchen (washing up, cleaning the floors, chopping vegetables etc.).

The scullion maid turned lady of the house made for a heart-warming love story in the Poldark *novels.*

~

Sedentary: Sedentary derives from the Latin verb *sedēre*, meaning to sit. Sedentary people tend to stay in the same place and not move around very much. A sedentary job requires sitting down all day, which can lead to a sedentary lifestyle and a lack of exercise that becomes detrimental to health.

Since retiring he had become very sedentary, rarely leaving the house and sitting for long hours in front of the television.

~

Senescent: In use since the late seventeenth century, senescent is the state of being old and derives from the Latin *senex*, meaning old. Other English words deriving from *senex* are senile, senior and senate.

Those in the care home mainly consisted of senescent residents.

≈

Sententious: A much-maligned word, sententious is often used in a negative fashion to describe a pompous windbag in love with their own opinions. Originally, the word, derived as it is from the Latin *sententia*, meant something meaningful, like a maxim or aphorism. Perhaps at some point people got bored of aphoristic language and decided that sententious should mean blustery and sanctimonious claptrap.

An apple a day keeps the doctor away is an example of a sententious statement.

≈

Sequacious: Sequacious derives from the Latin *sequac*, meaning somebody prone to follow. The word has similarities with being subservient, and although initially it was used to describe loyal subjects following their leader, over time it has come to mean a person who blindly follows without question or thought.

The sequacious actions of those involved in the bizarre cult carried accusations of brain-washing in the press.

≈

Serendipity: Meaning the finding of useful or interesting information by accident, serendipity was first coined in 1754 by the English author Horace Walpole. He invented the word after recalling a tale about the three princes of Serendip who, on their travels, repeatedly made inadvertent discoveries.

As if by serendipity, they came across their dream home while on holiday in France.

≈

Sesquipedalian: It makes sense that a word that means excessive use of long words, especially words with multiple syllables, should be an ungainly, barely pronounceable word. The Roman poet Horace coined the phrase *sesquipedalia verba* (meaning words a foot and a half long) in his critique of the art of writing, *Ars Poetica*. This may have been an ironic joke but plenty of haughty literary critics have taken the point on board and thrown accusations of sesquipedalian tendencies at writers they disapprove of.

I know people of good taste who rave about the author, but his sesquipedalian prose drives me mad.

~

Shaveling: A shaveling was a slightly disparaging term for somebody coerced into religious instruction and thereby forced to shave their heads. It could, however, be applied to anybody joining a group or cult that requires the shedding of hair as a symbol of membership.

It was alarming to see the number of youthful shavelings marching in support of right-wing extremism.

~

Shibboleth: In the biblical Book of Judges (12:4-6) there is a story that explains the origins of shibboleth. A Hebrew tribe, the Ephraimites, after they were defeated by the Gileadite army, tried to retreat by sneaking across a ford of the Jordan River that was held by their enemy. The Gileadites, wary of the ploy, asked every soldier who tried to cross if he was an Ephraimite. If the soldier replied no, he was asked to say 'shibboleth' (which means stream in Hebrew). Gileadites pronounced the word as 'shibboleth', but Ephraimites said it as 'sibboleth'. Anyone who left out the initial 'sh' was killed on the spot. When English speakers first borrowed shibboleth, they used it to mean a test phrase. Over time it came to mean a truism or platitude.

Time heals all wounds is a well-known shibboleth.

~

Sibilant: As an adjective, sibilant can be used to describe a hissing, low, whispered utterance. It has connotations of the sinister or darkly erotic. As a noun, sibilant refers simply to a sound in phonetics, namely a 'sh' (shuh) or 's'. It's peculiar, perhaps, that many writers are prone to use sibilant as an adjective to describe sensual-sounding speech when in reality their characters probably spoke with a lisp.

She blushed at the sibilant sound of his whispering overtures.

≈

Simulacrum: Closely linked to the word simulation (both words derive from the Latin *simulare*, meaning to copy), a simulacrum is an artificial representation of something real. Originally, the word related to direct copies, such as waxwork figures or portrait paintings, but over time it has come to be seen as a negative and artificial replacement for something real. Post-Structuralist philosophers such as Jean Baudrillard and Jacques Derrida adopted the word to describe the artificiality of modern cultural forms.

Reality TV is the ultimate, if oxymoronic, simulacrum of real life.

≈

Skirl: Anybody who has ever found the sound of bagpipes hard to take will appreciate the fact that the instrument has given rise to its own unique verb. To skirl is to make a sound from blowing into a set of bagpipes and, appropriately enough, at least for bagpipe detractors, the word derives from the Middle English word *skirlen*, meaning to shriek or scream.

Oh the dulcet skirl of the bagpipes is so redolent of the Highlands and the misty lochs.

≈

Skitter: Derived from the Old Norse *skyt*, meaning to move at pace, to skitter is used to mean something that moves in a quick and effortless, natural fashion.

The incoming tide crashed skittering waves on to the shoreline.

≈

Skulduggery: The origins of the word skulduggery, meaning underhanded or unscrupulous behaviour, are unknown, but it could possibly be derived from the word *sculduddery*, which used to be a term for gross or lewd conduct. Its first documented use was in the mid-nineteenth century.

He appeared to have amassed his fortune through skulduggery.

≈

Slake: To slake is to lessen the power or force of something, to abate a desire, ambition or incentive. The word is loosely related to the Old English *sleac*, meaning to slacken, which in modern times has a more negative connotation. Shakespeare used the word several times in his plays and poems.

'It could not slake mine ire, nor ease my heart.'

William Shakespeare, *Henry VI*, Part 3, Act 1, Scene 3

~

Solecism: The ancient city of Soloi is to blame for the word solecism. Cilicia was an ancient coastal nation in Asia Minor populated by Athenian colonists known as the *soloikos*. Legend has it that away from the cosmopolitan cultural influences of imperial Athens, the colonists of Soloi became quite lazy with their native language. As a result, *soloikos* gained a new meaning of speaking incorrectly. The Athenian Greeks used that sense as the basis of the phrase *soloikismos*, meaning an ungrammatical combination of words. The word solecism in English has the same meaning of deviating from the accepted norm, especially in relation to language but also sometimes in social situations.

The writer Penelope Lively once said she never reads her own books after they are published for fear they are riddled with solecisms.

~

Solemnity: In modern parlance solemnity means the state or quality of being serious and dignified. In the Middle Ages, however, solemnities were very formal and dignified ceremonies such as funerals, usually conducted by the Church.

The funeral passed with the requisite solemnity and sorrow.

~

Solicitous: Solicitous has its roots in the Latin word *sollicitus*, meaning anxious. This idea of anxiety, in a nice way, became concern for the welfare and well-being of others. A solicitous person is eager to help and often worries a lot.

The teacher was very solicitous about the welfare of her students.

~

Somnolence and Somnambulism: Somnolence is a state of drowsiness, moments just before sleeping, which may possibly lead to somnambulism – that is, sleepwalking.

The film was so dull I felt myself fighting against somnolence after twenty minutes.

~

Soporific: Another woozy word related to sleep. Soporific describes things that induce sleep or dull the senses into a sleep-like state.

I find putting classical music on the radio late at night has a soporific effect on me.

~

Sortilege: The historical term for the practice of predicting the future by deducing the random associations of objects or symbols as in tarot card reading or tea-leaves. The word derives from Old French/Latin; a *sorteligus* was a mystic or soothsayer in medieval France. Sortilège was also a name adopted by a French heavy metal band in the 1980s and a sickly sweet cocktail made from mixing whiskey with maple syrup, which originates from Quebec, Canada.

Many innocent people were burned at the stake by the Inquisition after being accused of sortilege.

~

Sough: An unusual word used to describe a low, soft murmuring sound, rather like a sigh but produced by natural causes such as a gentle breeze rustling leaves on a tree.

As she hugged the tree, the great old oak emitted a sorrowful sough.

~

Spruce: The first recorded use of spruce was in 1594 and it means to make something, or someone, neat, clean or stylish.

Before putting it on the market, they gave the house a coat of paint to spruce it up.

~

Stanch versus Staunch: The verb stanch, rarely used, but elegant nonetheless, is closely related to the adjective staunch. However, whereas staunch means steadfast and implacable, the verb to stanch means to check or stop the flow of something, such as tears, or blood from a wound. Both words derive from the Anglo-French word *estancher*, meaning to stop the flow, so it can only be assumed that staunch came after the flow had been stopped.

She was a staunch feminist who fought for women's rights throughout her life.

~

Statant: A word chiefly related to heraldry and the custom of having animals standing in profile (or statant) on coats of arms. The word is occasionally applied to models in photographs standing facing away from the camera.

I saw a beautiful photograph of Cindy Crawford in statant pose, used for a perfume company.

~

Stridulate, Stridulation and Stridulatory: Stridulate is one member of a word family that has its ancestry in the Latin word *stridulus*, meaning shrill. Also in this family is stridulation, a noun that can either refer to the shrill sound made when an insect stridulates (rubs together bodily parts to produce sound – like the noise made by crickets and grasshoppers) or can simply mean the act of stridulating. Another *stridulus* word is stridulatory, which means able to stridulate; not all insects can.

The sound of the stridulating crickets kept me awake all night.

~

Stultify versus Nullify: As late as the 1890s, to stultify someone was to make them appear foolish and stupid. The word was used often in reports of court cases where witnesses or defendants were tied in knots through aggressive questioning by bullying barristers. By the mid-twentieth century, however, stultify came to mean to have a dulling or inhibiting effect, such as the stultifying impact of the sun on very hot days, causing people to feel lethargic. Stultify is also sometimes used as a synonym for nullify, but this is a mistake. To nullify something is to make it of no value or consequence or to deaden the effect or outcome of a situation.

I didn't see much of Madrid while I was visiting because the heat in July is so stultifying.

The defence were able to nullify the attacking threat posed by the opposition's forwards.

~

Succour: The Latin verb *succurrere*, meaning to rush to the aid of, is the root of this word that has existed in English since the Middle Ages. It can be used as a verb, as in 'to succour a situation by helping', but such usage is rare. Typically, the term is used as a noun; thus we speak of providing succour by way of relief or aid.

It is a moral duty to provide succour to those in extreme poverty.

~

Supernal: Something that belongs in the heavens or the sky can be described as supernal. The word is often used to describe star quality in a performance by an actor or musician.

The supernal quality of the orchestra's rendition had the audience in raptures.

~

Supine: The Latin word *supīnus*, meaning to lie face up or flat on one's back, is the root for the adjective supine. Over time a secondary meaning beyond physical posture has arisen, which suggests weakness and inertia. A supine response to something is literally taking things lying down in a figurative sense.

The supine response to recent setbacks spoke volumes about the CEO's leadership skills.

~

Susurration: A susurration is like a whisper but is composed not of words but of low, murmuring or humming sounds. It is light and gentle and often associated with nature, such as the rustling of leaves or of wind gently whistling through trees.

The music slowly diminished until all that remained were low, tinkering susurrations of sound.

~

Syzygy: One of a select group of words in English not containing a vowel, syzygy is the straight-line configuration of three celestial bodies, such as the sun, moon and earth, during a solar or lunar eclipse.

We walked up to the top of the hill to try to get a good view of the syzygy but it had clouded over.

T

~

Tacit versus Taciturn: The Latin word *tacēre*, meaning to be silent, is the root of both these words, although there is a subtle deviation in meaning. A tacit agreement is something understood without being formally stated in words. A taciturn person is disinclined to talk, either due to temperament or confidence.

Normally taciturn and withdrawn, he became much more positive and talkative after a few drinks.

~

Tamp: To tamp something down is often used interchangeably with the expression 'damp down', meaning to lessen in effect or importance. As a verb, tamp first appeared in written English in the early 1800s. It was used specifically in mining to refer both to putting an explosive charge into a borehole, and to packing the borehole with clay or earth before detonating the charge. This meaning still exists in construction: the tamping of concrete, for example (packing down into a mould). However, by the mid-twentieth century to tamp something down also developed the same meaning as to damp down.

The manager was eager to tamp down supporters' expectations.

~

Taradiddle: One of a number of words related to nonsense for which the source or derivation is unknown. Taradiddle first appeared in English in a dictionary of colloquial slang, where it was defined as a lie or untruth. Over time the word has taken on the meaning of poppycock and balderdash.

A succession of wild accusations were dismissed as utter taradiddle.

~

Tartuffe: The French dramatist Molière is responsible for this word for an imposter or hypocrite, especially someone pretending to be pious and upstanding. Tartuffe is the principal character in Molière's 1664 comedy of the same name, which concerns the misadventures of a man pretending to be virtuous to further his own desires.

I wasn't taken in by his claims of religious conversion and had him earmarked as a Tartuffe all along.

~

Tatterdemalion: The origin of tatterdemalion is unclear but the word has been in the English language since the early seventeenth century. The word is suggestive of tattered scraps of cloth and it is used as a noun to describe someone of ragged and ill-kempt appearance and clothing.

Despite his often tatterdemalion appearance, he was actually a very wealthy man.

~

Tautology: Tautology, deriving from the Greek *tautologos* and meaning needless repetition of an idea, statement or word, was first documented in the English language in 1566.

The salesman's use of tautology bored my wife who was tired of hearing about the car's advantages over and over again.

~

Tectonic: Tectonic is a geological term used to describe processes related to the structure of the earth's crust. We speak, for example, of tectonic plates, the movement of which causes earthquakes and mountain building. It has also come to be used to describe a drastic shift that has a strong and widespread impact.

There was a tectonic shift in societal values in the late 1960s.

~

Temulence and Temulent: Temulence is a state of extreme drunkenness, and the adjective temulent is a rather quaint description of rowdy drunken behaviour.

The soccer fans were fairly well behaved at first, but as the beer flowed, the more temulent their behaviour became.

~

Tenebrosity: The Latin word for darkness is *tenebrosus*. Tenebrosity is the quality of gloominess and suggests a sombre and dingy atmosphere.

The film was darkly lit at times, adding to an overall effect of tenebrosity.

~

Tergiversate and Tergiversation: The Latin verb *tergiversari* means to show reluctance, and it comes from the combination of *tergum*, meaning back, and *versare*, meaning to turn. The verb and noun relate to somebody who is pointedly evasive and makes conflicting comments or statements. Or, in a political context, someone who makes a sudden U-turn from a previously stated position or principle.

Her ability to tergiversate gave ammunition to her opponents.

~

Terrene: The Latin word for earth, *terra*, gives us the adjective terrene. It is something that is earthy and stable, almost to the point of being mundane and dull.

Her boyfriend's dependable, stable and terrene outlook had begun to bore her, as she yearned to be with someone with more ambition.

～

Theopneustic: If a person experiences a theopneustic intervention, they have been touched by the hand or spirit of God. This word, deriving from the Greek *theos*, for God, and *pneuma*, meaning spirit, denotes a direct experience of what is taken to be divine intervention.

Maradona gave a sly, theopneustic explanation for cheating against England in the 1986 World Cup.

～

Theriac: Derived from the Greek word *theriaca*, meaning a potion that cures all, a theriac is a dubious potion designed to treat any possible illness or disease. The first theriac was supposedly created by the first-century Greek physician Andromachus, whose concoction consisted of some seventy drugs pulverized with honey. Theriacs were particularly popular in the Middle Ages during periods of plague.

The drink Benedictine was originally developed as a theriac and elixir of long life.

～

Thimblerig and Thimblerigger: Thimblerig is a word from the Victorian era that relates to a 'street game' in which a small pea is hidden under one of three thimbles and swapped around at speed. Spectators are then invited to guess which thimble is hiding the pea. The performers of this well-known trick were known as thimbleriggers.

I lost five pounds to a thimblerigger at the fairground.

～

Thraldom: Thraldom is the word for the state of being in servitude or under the power of another person, as in enslaved.

The Thirteenth Amendment of the US Constitution effectively abolished the principles of thraldom in the United States.

~

Timocracy versus Plutocracy: A timocracy (from the Greek *timē*, meaning price or worth, and *kratia*, meaning rule) is a state in which only property owners may participate in government. The more extreme forms of timocracy, where power derives entirely from wealth with no regard for social or civic responsibility, may shift in their form and become a plutocracy, in which the wealthy and powerful use their power to increase their wealth.

The fact that the richest 1 per cent own over half the world's wealth is tantamount to timocracy.

~

Timorous: Timorous derives from the Latin verb *timēre*, meaning to fear. A timorous person is usually easily frightened and fearful.

She took hesitant, timorous steps along the dark corridor.

~

Tintinnabulation and Tinnitus: The Latin verb *tintinnare* means to jingle or ring, hence tintinnabulation is the sound of bells. The debilitating condition of tinnitus (ringing or buzzing in the inner ear) derives from the same root.

'. . . the tintinnabulation that so musically wells
From the bells, bells, bells, bells,
Bells, bells, bells
From the jingling and the tinkling of the bells.'

Edgar Allan Poe, *The Bells* (1849)

~

Titillate: The original meaning of titillate was to lightly stroke a sensitive part of the body so as to provoke a reaction, most usually laughter. Titillate was therefore synonymous with tickling. The word, while retaining its general meaning of exciting the senses, has come to denote something that incites feelings of sexual desire or eroticism.

The excessive nudity in the film seemed cynically designed to titillate teenage boys and added little to the narrative.

～

Titivate: When we titivate something, we spruce it up and make it smarter or more eye-catching, often by making small but significant alterations.

He titivated his attire for the wedding by adding a smart cravat.

～

Titubant: Derived from the French word for faltering, titubant describes a staggering or stumbling movement, possibly due to intoxication. It is related to an Italian word *titubante*, which describes somebody who dithers and is indecisive in their actions.

He looked the worse for wear and was lurching along the road in a titubant manner.

～

Tontine: A tontine is a financial investment scheme whereby the participants usually contribute equally to a prize that is awarded to whichever participant survives all the others. The word is named after a Neapolitan banker, Lorenzo de Tonti. In 1653, Tonti persuaded investors to buy shares in a fund he had created. Each year, the investors earned dividends, and when one of them died, his or her share of the profits were redistributed among the survivors. When the last investor died, the capital reverted to the state.

Tontine schemes are banned in some US states due to fears of corruption, fraud and skulduggery.

～

Torpor: Torpor first appeared in written English in a thirteenth-century guide for religious recluses, where it referred to a spiritual or intellectual lethargy. The modern meaning of torpor covers both physical and mental sluggishness.

The winter months saw him descend into a state of apathy and torpor.

~

Tortuous versus Torturous: Tortuous and torturous are commonly used interchangeably although their meanings are quite distinct. Both words derive from the Latin verb *torquere*, meaning to twist or to wind, and the problem lies in exactly what the speaker is trying to describe. For example, 'a tortuous hike up the mountain' means a pathway that was winding and crooked. However 'a torturous hike up the mountain' means the walk was so arduous it was akin to torture.

He gave a long, elaborate and tortuous explanation, which was torturous to listen to.

~

Traduce: Traduce is one of a number of English synonyms that means to injure by speaking ill of. Traduce is suggestive of a deliberate attempt to damage a person's reputation, possibly through false accusations and lies.

Tabloid newspapers traduced his reputation with a series of scandalous accusations.

~

Trammel: To trammel something is to attempt to thwart or impede it in some way, or to hold it back or obstruct. A trammel is also a type of fishing net, which gives the word its secondary meaning of becoming enmeshed in something.

A committee has been set up to report against any further proposals to trammel the rights of casual workers.

~

Tramontane: Tramontane came into English via Italian. The Italian word *tramontano* is formed of *trans*, meaning to cross, and *montanus*, meaning mountain. Someone described as *tramontane*, therefore, was a person from the other side of the mountain. The meaning in English remained more or less the same for a couple of hundred years before gradually expanding to mean any foreigner, regardless of their proximity to mountains.

He returned from his travels with an exotic, tramontane wife in tow.

∾

Transilience and Transilient: The noun form, transilience, is a geological term relating to sudden changes in rock formations and structures. As an adjective, transilient can be used to describe abrupt changes or variations within a set structure.

Monument Valley in the United States is noted for its geological transilience.

∾

Transmute: Something transmutes when it changes from one form into another, altering its appearance and nature. Writers can transmute their life experiences into fiction and musicians can take a popular song and transmute it by changing its tempo or key. Some religions believe in the transmutation of human consciousness (e.g. Buddhism) or the transmutation of the soul into other forms after death.

Johnny Cash transmuted the form of several classic songs in his American Songbook series of albums.

∾

Trenchant: The word trenchant comes from the Anglo-French verb *trencher*, meaning to cut. Hence, a trenchant sword is one with a very sharp edge; a trenchant remark is one that cuts deep; and a trenchant observation is one that cuts to the heart of the matter.

He delivered a withering analysis peppered with pertinent and trenchant observations.

~

Triturate: In chemistry to triturate a substance is to crush or grind it into a fine powder so that it can be dissolved into a solution. In a wider sense, our teeth triturate food so that it can be swallowed and better digested.

After the accident I found it difficult to triturate solid food and had to be served up liquefied meals.

~

Trivium and Quadrivium: In medieval education and learning, seven liberal arts were deemed worthy of study. The trivium was considered the lower level of study and was comprised of grammar, logic and rhetoric. The quadrivium was considered the higher level of study and consisted of arithmetic, geometry, astrology and music. Both words derive from the Latin word for crossroads: the point where three roads meet (*trivium*) or four (*quadrivium*).

They created a trivium by combining all three theories together.

~

Truckle: A truckle at one time was a small wheel attached to beds so that they could moved around and easily stored. These beds became known as truckle beds. Often used by children, they were stored under larger beds for adults. This gave rise to the figurative sense of truckle as being subservient to someone larger or more prominent, or bending to their will in an obsequious manner.

He was obsessed by wealth and status and would truckle up to anyone he thought had power and influence.

~

Turpitude: The Latin word *turpitudo* comes from *turpis*, which means vile or base. The word is often heard in the phrase 'moral turpitude', an expression used in law to designate an act or behaviour that gravely violates the sentiment or accepted standards of the community.

People convicted of crimes of moral turpitude in Alabama automatically lose the right to vote.

~

Tyro: Derived from the Latin *tiro*, which means young soldier, new recruit, or more generally a novice, a tyro is somebody who is new to (often young) or inexperienced in an endeavour or position. The word can be spelt with either a 'y' or an 'i' (as in the original Latin).

The tyro conductor put in a promising performance.

U

~

Uberty: Derived from the Middle French word *uberté*, meaning abundance, and closely linked to the German word *über*, meaning above or over, uberty refers to any crop or harvest that has been particularly fertile and fruitful.

The warm autumn meant an uberty of wild blackberries sprouting in the hedgerows.

~

Ubiety: The condition of being placed in a particular location or relative position as in, for example, the ubiety of words in a sentence.

After changing jobs I no longer had the luxurious ubiety of being able to work from home.

~

Ubiquitous: Deriving from the Latin word *ubique*, ubiquitous means to be everywhere at the same time, something popular and constantly encountered. Ubiquity first appeared in print in the late sixteenth century but ubiquitous does not appear to have been used until around 1874.

Mobile phones have become ubiquitous and it's very rare to come across someone who doesn't own one.

~

Ukase: A word that has its roots in French and Russian and means an order from above. A Russian *ukase* was a command from the highest levels of government that could not be disobeyed. By the early nineteenth century, English speakers were also using ukase generally for any command that seemed to come from a higher authority, particularly one that was final or arbitrary.

Given the management's ukase, no one dared to challenge established procedure.

⁓

Uliginous and Uliginal: A botanical term for any plant that grows in wetlands or swamps or generally damp habitats.

The uliginal plants that grow in wetlands provide the perfect environment for many insects and amphibians.

⁓

Ullage: Ullage is the amount of space left in a tank or container after some of the liquid or substance has been taken out, leaked or been used.

I used to mark the ullage line on bottles of wine to stop my housemates from helping themselves.

⁓

Ulotrichous: The quality of having tightly curled, woolly hair is described as ulotrichous.

She was very proud of her long locks of red ulotrichous hair.

⁓

Ultraism: This denotes the doctrine of advocating extreme measures or courses of action during a conflict or political and social upheaval. Ultraism is another word for the more currently in vogue term 'radicalism'.

All schools are working hard to identify instances of ultraism.

⁓

Umbrage: Originally, umbrage meant shadow or shade, *umbra* being the Latin word for shade. Over time the word came to be attached to shadowy or shady actions or behaviour. Shakespeare uses this sense of sinister goings on in *Hamlet* (see quote below). Understandably, when a person's shady behaviour is found out, someone is likely to take offence, and it is from this that the modern meaning of umbrage developed.

> *'... his semblable is his mirror. And who else would trace him? His umbrage, nothing more.'*
>
> William Shakespeare, *Hamlet*, Act 5, Scene 3

~

Unction versus Unctuous: Unction is derived from the Latin word *unguere*, meaning to anoint. In religious ceremonies, ointments made from essences and oils from plants were often used for ceremonies and healing rituals, and these became known as unctions. It is from this that the adjective unctuous developed and began to be applied to people of an oily or slippery manner. An unctuous person is typically flattering and ingratiating, but in a way that seems insincere and false.

> *The unctuous manner of the hotel owner became quite grating.*

~

Uneath: In Old English something described as *ēathe* was something straightforward and easy. The opposite of *ēathe* was *unēathe*, something tricky or complex. It is from these words that the adjective uneath developed, to mean a difficult action or task.

> *In diving, points are awarded according to the degree of difficulty of the dives – the more uneath the manoeuvre, the higher the score.*

~

Unedifying: Something unedifying is usually of little moral or intellectual value or stimulation. The word can also mean generally negative and unpleasant.

> *The novel paints a bleak and unedifying picture of the future of humanity.*

~

Unfeigned versus Feigned: We think of the verb to feign as to pretend, but in Shakespeare's time to feign had the meaning of insincerity, particularly in matters of the heart. Unfeigned, then, is used to describe something sincere and truthful.

> *'No, truly, for the truest poetry is the most feigning, and lovers are given to poetry, and what they swear in poetry may be said as lovers they do feign.'*
>
> William Shakespeare, *As You Like It*, Act 3, Scene 3

She gazed at him, her eyes full of unfeigned admiration.

~

Unguiculate, Unguiferous and Unguiform: The Latin word for fingernails is *unguiculus*, and it is from this that the following string of scratchy adjectives springs. Unguiculate is a creature that is clawed; unguiferous is the action of baring claws in an aggressive manner; and unguiform is something that is shaped like a claw.

The animal bared its teeth and looked ready to launch an unguiferous attack.

~

Unpropitious: Unpropitious often relates to what may commonly be known as bad timing. In Latin *propitius* meant favourably inclined, and it was linked in part to the superstitious notion that good and bad luck is influenced by the alignment of the stars. Unpropitious relates to the negative side, and suggests that something seems unlikely to be resolved in a positive way.

It was an unpropitious time to call an election, so the government clung to power for several more years.

~

Upbraid: To upbraid someone is to severely scold and reproach them for their faults or behaviour. The Old English word *upbrēdan*, meaning to find fault, is the root, but generally people are upbraided on account of their actions.

His wife upbraided him for his drinking and gambling habits.

~

Urticate, Urtication and Urticaria: *Urticare* in medieval Latin meant to sting, or be stung by something, usually an insect, hence to urticate. This has given rise to two closely linked nouns. Urtication is a skin irritation, generally symptomatic of an allergic reaction to food and involving itching and redness of skin and breaking out in hives. Urticaria is the official medical term for the aforementioned reactions.

I can't eat shellfish as it provokes severe urticaria on my face.

~

Usufruct: The concept behind usufruct comes from the Latin phrase *usus et fructus,* or use and enjoyment. When granted the right of usufruct, an individual has the right to use and enjoy the fruits or assets of property belonging to another person.

Although not given possession of my uncle's villa in his will, I was granted usufruct rights to visit and stay whenever I please.

~

Usury: Usury is the rather grubby lending of money with an interest charge for its use. It is generally used in a negative sense to describe barely legal charges of exorbitant interest rates.

Payday loan companies have been widely accused of usury.

~

Uxorious: This is a rather curiously negative adjective in that uxorious means excessive devotion and sentimental attachment to one's wife. It is, however, often used mildly disparagingly to describe somebody slavishly devoted and subservient through their doting.

He had thoroughly uxorious opinions of his wife.

V

Vacillate: To vacillate is to switch between different, often opposing positions in either thought, opinion or action. A secondary meaning is to sway between different conditions due to a lack of equilibrium, as with the weather.

The minister's political reputation was damaged by his tendency to vacillate on key policy decisions.

Vacuous versus Vacuity: The Latin adjective *vacuus*, meaning empty, provides the stem for both these words. However, whereas vacuous is usually applied to people marked by a lack of ideas or intelligence, a vacuity is simply an empty space.

Every time he was asked a question at the press conference his responses were vacuous.

Valediction: A sombre word for sorrowful moments. Valediction, put simply, is the act of saying goodbye, and is often used to describe eulogies at funeral ceremonies, but it can also be used in the context of any farewell or final speech.

'I'm just going outside and may be some time,' said Oates, by way of valediction.

Valetudinarian: To describe somebody as a valetudinarian sounds quite grandiose and important. However, valetudinarians are the scourge of health professionals because of their morbid obsession with illness, and in extreme cases, death. It's an alternative word for a hypochondriac.

Although in generally good health, his grandmother was prone to play the valetudinarian whenever she felt under the weather.

~

Vaticinate and Vaticinator: The ability to vaticinate, at least with some degree of accuracy, is a useful skill. The word derives from Latin and roughly translates as the act of singing about the future. In modern usage it is a slightly highbrow word for the act of making predictions. Hence a vaticinator, in noun form, is someone who forecasts future events.

He lost his job as a horseracing tipster on account of his chronic inability to vaticinate race results correctly.

~

Vehement: A not unusual word commonly associated with impassioned arguments, vehement is a flexible adjective that can be used to describe any words or actions that are forthright and strong.

The audience rose as one at the end of the performance and demanded several curtain calls from the cast with minutes of vehement applause.

~

Verbiage: An ironic inclusion in this book, verbiage derives from French (via Old French) and means to chatter or ramble in speech or writing. There is often a negative connotation, as someone guilty of verbiage uses far too many words, generally in a superfluous and/ or pretentious manner.

He liked to hold court at dinner parties but was oblivious to the fact that his verbiage was far from engaging.

~

Verdant: A hybrid of the Old French, *vert*, meaning the colour green, and *virērē* from Latin, meaning to be green in colour or aspect, verdant is most commonly used to describe rich and lush naturally green environments. A secondary meaning, common in the eighteenth century but scarcely used today, is to denote a person who is inexperienced in a particular activity or endeavour.

The manager's talented young team, although verdant, put on a performance of great promise for the future.

∽

Verecund: Verecund derives from the Latin word *verecundus,* which relates to a person who is shy, bashful and modest. It is rarely used in modern English, but *verecondo* in Italian and *verecundo* in Portuguese have the same meaning and are much more prevalent in general speech and writing in these countries.

My friend's two sons had contrasting personalities. The youngest was boisterous and energetic while the eldest was quiet and verecund.

∽

Verisimilitude: The easiest way to remember the meaning of verisimilitude is to tweak the word into the phrase 'very similar to'. It is an unusual word as, by rights, it should be an adjective, but it functions instead as an uncountable noun. The degree of verisimilitude something has relates to how close it is to real life or how much it appears to be real.

Computer-generated images have become so sophisticated that cinema audiences are often fooled by their verisimilitude.

∽

Vernal: *Ver* is the Latin word for spring, so anything that is vernal is related to or occurs during springtime. Vernal flowers, the vernal equinox, vernal rain showers and, in ancient times, the ghoulish practice of the *ver sacrum* (child sacrifice to the gods to protect the harvest) can all be described as vernal. More poetically, it can be used of people to evoke the callowness of youth.

In Arthur Rimbaud, the poet Paul Verlaine finally found the vernal muse he desired.

∽

Vertiginous: Derived from the word vertigo and descended from the Latin verb *vertere,* meaning to spin or turn, vertiginous relates mainly to anything liable to induce dizziness or make the head spin. The word is often used in the context of steep heights, such as 'the vertiginous Cliffs of Moher' in Ireland. Other figurative uses of vertiginous describe sudden and spectacular descents or drops, such as a vertiginous fall in the stock market. Less commonly, somebody who is prone to making sudden and often pointless decisions could be said to be acting vertiginously.

Following the company's admission that it was bankrupt, there was a vertiginous drop in company morale.

~

Vespertine and Vespertilian: The Latin word *vesper* means evening. From this the adjectives vespertine and vespertilian derive. The former has the sense of something that comes alive in the evenings, or that is of the evening. Vespertilian relates to any aspect that may be considered bat-like, for bats sleep during the day and fly at night.

The small town appeared very sleepy, but has a vespertine quality and is positively buzzing after sundown.

My teenage son has vespertilian tendencies; it's a struggle to get him to do anything during the day but he gets very hyperactive at night.

~

Vicarious(ly): A word that can be used in various contexts. To experience something vicariously is usually to gain pleasure from observing or receiving information about another person's actions and behaviour. Alternative meanings are: replacing another person in a particular action or situation; being held to account for another's actions, as in the case of vicarious punishment; or delegating authority – put simply, asking another person to make decisions on your behalf.

The men in the pub derived vicarious pleasure from the wild tales of the landlord's sexual exploits.

~

Viduage: The state of widowhood or becoming a widow.

The duchess thought it prudent to maintain her viduage for no less than two years from the day of the duke's passing.

~

Vilipend: The verb to vilipend first appeared in English in the fifteenth century from the Middle French/Latin term *vilis*, which was used to describe something tawdry or vile. Transformed into a verb, therefore, it means to treat somebody with contempt, or to slander and vilify in speech or writing.

There is a tradition among the gutter press to vilipend successful people, especially if they are from working-class backgrounds.

~

Visceral: In its strictest sense visceral relates to the *viscera* (from Latin), the internal organs of the human body (heart, liver, intestines etc.). However, visceral is often used in a figurative sense to describe a deep or intuitive feeling, or a gut reaction to a situation or event.

The terrible loss of life caused by the tsunami provoked a visceral reaction in many people across the world.

~

Vitiate: To vitiate something is to debase or spoil it through actions or words. Like the word vituperative (see below), it stems from the Latin noun *vitium*, which relates to vices or faults. Vitiate is also prevalent in legal language to describe an agreement or contract that has become spoiled through actions or circumstances.

While some people don't appear to care about wildlife, we can't allow that to vitiate the integrity of the majority.

~

Vitreous: A vitreous object is one either made of, or resembling glass in aspect or manner. There is also a medical noun related to the adjective, the vitreous humour, which denotes the transparent jelly-like liquid inside the eyeball – hence the description 'glassy eyed'.

The lake was so still it took on a vitreous quality.

~

Vituperative: Although sharing the same Latin stem as vitiate, vituperative relates in particular to utterances that are severely disapproving, censorious and/or abusive. Perhaps at some point to scold and abuse other people publicly was regarded as a vice or a fault.

There was considerable apprehension within the White House over the president's vituperative use of Twitter.

Voluble: From the Latin *volubilis*, meaning winding or rolling, voluble describes somebody who speaks in a fluent and seemingly effortless style. Many words are used to describe talkative people, such as loquacious, garrulous and verbose (see also Verbiage), but only voluble describes somebody for whom words roll off their tongue.

A naturally voluble man, he was adept at public speaking.

Votive: Votive offerings or dedications express a wish or a vow. It is common practice to light votive candles in churches and temples in dedication to loved ones or the departed.

Crowds gathered in the main square carrying votive candles.

W

Wadi: The Arabic word *wadi* describes the bed or valley of a stream in the desert, often hidden underground. Wadis are found in regions of southwestern Asia and northern Africa. They are dry for most of the year, except during the rainy season when they often form an oasis.

We visited a desert oasis that had sprung up around a wadi when we went on holiday to Tunisia.

~

Wassail: The Vikings liked to party (when they weren't too busy raping and pillaging or burning down villages) and the word wassail derives from the Old Norse drinking toast of *ves heill*, meaning be healthy. This phrase mutated into Old English as wassail and, over time, became the name for a type of warm drink, typically drunk at Christmas, not dissimilar to mulled wine or mulled cider.

This year, rather than serving mulled wine I looked up a recipe for a traditional English wassail as an alternative.

~

Waygoose: The waygoose (sometimes spelt wayzgoose) relates to a tradition dating back to the late seventeenth century. Once a year, printers' guilds would put on a huge feast for their staff, involving much revelry, entertainment and merriment, this being known as a waygoose. By the nineteenth century the tradition had declined but it had a revival in the twentieth century where the waygoose became typically a company daytrip. The modern equivalent of the waygoose is either the office away-day or the company Christmas party.

When the boss said he was planning on taking us all out on a waygoose, we had no idea what he was talking about.

~

Wayment: To wayment over something is to lament or grieve its passing or loss, typically the death of a loved one.

After the sudden death of her father she struggled to wayment and find closure.

~

Welkin: This word relating to the heavens has been used in English to refer to the vault of the sky since at least the twelfth century and derives from an earlier word from Old English, *wolcen*, which meant cloud. In modern English it is often used to express exuberance of emotion, like cries from the heavens. Interestingly, the original words of the popular Christmas carol 'Hark! The Herald Angels Sing' was 'Hark how all the welkin rings'.

> *'The sun of heaven, methought, was loath to set,*
> *But stay'd and made the western welkin blush.'*
>
> <div align="right">William Shakespeare, <i>King John</i>, Act 5, Scene 5</div>

∾

Weltschmerz: Derived from the German word for the world, *welt*, and *schmerz*, meaning pain, weltschmerz was born during the gloomy era of the Romantic poets. The German writer Jean Paul (pseudonym of Johann Paul Friedrich Richter) first coined the phrase in his 1827 novel *Selina*, and it describes a sense of weariness and depression that the way of the world in reality is far from an idealized vision of how it could be – hence 'world-pain'.

> *I often suffer dreadful feelings of weltschmerz when watching the evening news bulletins.*

∾

Wergild: Originally set in Anglo-Saxon and Germanic law, wergild was a fine that the family of a murderer was forced to pay to the family of their victim as a form of compensation.

> *Compensation for the victims of violent crime is a form of modern-day wergild.*

∾

Wertfreiheit: A complex word from German that relates to critical analysis in the sciences and social sciences, Wertfreiheit roughly translates as free from value judgements. In short: it is not fair to believe that statements are correct because they correspond to one's own value system (opinions, ideas, ideals) or false because they do not.

> *Wertfreiheit is an attempt to protect neutrality in empirical studies.*

∾

Whelm: To be whelmed is to be quietly satisfied with something. However, whelmed originally meant what we now understand as being overwhelmed – that is, overcome with joy and emotion (or sadness and grief). Underwhelmed developed later than either whelmed or overwhelmed, bringing with it a negative sense of being dissatisfied and mildly disappointed. As a result, whelmed has shifted to being neither under nor over, but just right.

I was whelmed to bump into an old friend in the street.

∾

Whereof versus Whereon: Two easily confused relative adverbs. Whereof means the subject of which I wish to speak. Whereon means on which place or thing I am describing in terms of physical location.

'Whereof one cannot speak, thereof one must be silent.'
Ludwig Wittgenstein, *Tractus Logico-Philosophicus* (1922)

To visit the temples of Egypt is to glimpse the foundations whereon the age of the great pharaohs was built.

∾

Wherret: An archaic, dialectal term for receiving a good old-fashioned clip or slap round the side of the head.

My dad used to say, 'Do that again and I'll wherret you', but he never did.

∾

Widdershins: Legend holds that demons always approached the devil widdershins. Not surprisingly, such a path was considered evil and unlucky. By the sixteenth century, English speakers had adopted the term (from the Old High German *widar*, meaning back or against, and *sinnen*, meaning to travel) for anything following a path opposite to the direction the sun travels across the sky.

Don't be dancing widdershins around me; it's the mark of the devil.

∾

Williwaw: A williwaw is a sudden violent gust of cold land air, common along mountainous coastal regions of high latitude. The origin of the word is unknown but it is believed to have been a sailing term coined by British maritime men and used initially to describe the inclement and unpredictable winds around the hazardous Magellan Straits in South America.

A sudden williwaw blew up from nowhere and wrecked the campsite.

～

Wiseacre: A word that sounds as if it derived from American street slang, wiseacre has existed in English since the sixteenth century, albeit with a slightly different meaning. The word derives from the Middle Dutch *wijssegger*, meaning soothsayer or mystic. When people realized that soothsayers were mostly frauds and conmen, the term wiseacre began to develop the sense of somebody who thinks or pretends they are clever but they aren't.

She was impressed by his intellect at first, but quickly realized he was merely a wiseacre.

～

Witling: This is a companion word to wiseacre, and emerged in English around the same period, although its roots are in the Old English word *witan* – meaning to know. A witling, however, doesn't know, or at least has little self-knowledge, for it refers to somebody who thinks they are amusing when they aren't.

There's a witling in every office, usually a man who lives alone and drives everyone mad with his inane jokes and comments.

～

Wittol: A rarely used archaic word that describes a man who is tolerant of his wife's infidelities, and acquiesces to the situation without complaint.

Cleopatra brought ruin to Caesar and later Mark Anthony, making wittols of them both.

～

Wormwood: Wormwood is a European plant that provides the active ingredient in the drink absinthe – a dark bitter green oil extract from which derives the drink's potency. The bitterness of the taste gives a clue to the figurative use of wormwood to describe a situation that is grievous or ill-tempered.

The bad-tempered game left both teams with the taste of wormwood in their mouths.

Writhled: A rarely used adjective but one not without its charms. Writhled is synonymous with other words like wrinkled and shrivelled but is perhaps closest to wizened as it relates mostly to ageing, lived-in, faces.

His writhled face broke into a smile as he recalled his Navy days.

Wynd: In Scottish English a wynd is a narrow street or alley between streets. Scotland is known for its often inclement weather and the word probably derives from the wind (wynd) whistling down these slender thoroughfares.

The older parts of Edinburgh have some delightful little wynds.

X

Xenophobe: Used to describe those who are unduly fearful of the concept of 'foreign' and, especially, people of foreign origin, the word xenophobe first came into use in 1922. It partially derives from the Greek noun *xenos*, meaning stranger, guest or foreigner. It is not technically a phobia at all but rather denotes someone who is narrow-minded, bigoted and racist.

He was labelled a xenophobe by his opponents.

Xerophagy: Deriving from both the Latin and Greek *xerophagia*, meaning to eat dried food only, xerophagy is the name given to the Christian practice in Eastern churches of strict fasting during Lent or Holy Week. No meat, fish, milk, cheese, butter, oil, wine, seasonings or spices may be consumed, with the practitioners surviving on only bread, salt, water and vegetables.

I'm sorry but I am participating in xerophagy at this time and therefore will not be able to accept your invitation to dinner.

Y

Yammer: Derived from the Old English *geomrian*, to be sad, and subsequently Middle English *yameren*, yammer has been used since the fifteenth century to describe repeated cries of distress or sorrow. It also means to complain or whine persistently.

The children yammered because the internet had gone down and they couldn't watch their favourite show on Netflix.

Yawp: Yawp, meaning to call out, yelp or to boast, first appeared in the English language in the fourteenth century and is derived from the Middle English *yolpen* or *yelpen*. It implies a squawking, yelping, rather irritating type of complaining, but has an element of silliness as it also means raucous noise.

If you desist from yawping about it you may be able to think of a solution to the predicament.

Yegg: This word was first used in New York in 1903, to describe a safecracker or robber. By 1905 the term yegg men had been adopted by the press to describe criminal gangs.

Overnight, the bank was robbed by a gang of yegg men.

~

Yogi: The first known use of the word yogi in the English language was in 1613. It means a person who practises or follows the philosophy of Yoga, or possibly a mystical and reflective person.

The yogi's followers hang on his every word.

Z

~

Zenith: Originating from Arabic and meaning the way over one's head, by the 1300s zenith was used to describe the highest point in the heavens and by the 1600s it had come to include other high points. Nowadays it is used to describe reaching the top of one's career.

When she played Desdemona she realized that she had reached the zenith of her theatrical aspirations.

~

Zephyr: Zephyr, a gentle breeze from the west, derives its name from Zephyrus, the Greek god of the west wind, and was used by both Chaucer and Shakespeare in a figurative and metaphorical sense. More recently, zephyr has been adopted as a term for a lightweight fabric and the clothing made from it.

As they walked along the beach they felt the soft zephyr on their faces.